Swords Into Plowshares

by

Ron Paul

also by Ron Paul:

Swords Into Plowshares

A Life in Wartime and a Future of Peace and Prosperity

by Ron Paul

Ron Paul Institute
FOR PEACE AND PROSPERITY
WWW.RONPAULINSTITUTE.ORG
833 W. Plantation Dr. ◆ Clute, TX 77531

ISBN: 978-0-9964265-0-3

Dedicated to a new generation that seeks peace and rejects the notion of inevitable war.

Special thanks to:

Adam Dick: Editing
Cynthia Fedler: Layout and Cover Design
Daniel McAdams: Managing Editor

Contents

There must be lights burning brighter somewhere
Got to be birds flying higher in a sky more blue
If I can dream of a better land
Where all my brothers walk hand in hand
Tell me why, oh why, oh why can't my dream come true?

"If I Can Dream" Elvis Presley

1

Growing Up With War

I was born in 1935. I do not recall a time when war was not being discussed.

December 7, 1941—the day the Japanese military attacked Pearl Harbor—is not etched in my memory. I was six years old then. But the memories of the next three and half years of continued war talk are still vivid.

My dad was an air raid warden. His job on all air raid drills was to sound the siren in our area of town. Though my four brothers and I may not have known the full significance of a potential attack, we all knew that the sirens, easily reachable by any of us, were never to be touched.

During an air raid drill, all lights were absolutely turned off, and the family sat around a console radio listening for news of the certainty that it was all just practice. The siren would then sound again, more softly, as an all-clear signal.

War is death and suffering

None of my brothers were old enough to be drafted; two uncles and several cousins were. Though my dad had three brothers, only one was drafted since the others were permitted to continue to operate the family dairy business. His drafted brother served in the Seabees on the island of Saipan in the Pacific. My mother's brother was also drafted. He was sent to Africa. Both returned after the war. Neither one saw combat.

I well understood what going to war meant.

Several members of the Lutheran church my family attended were drafted and sent to Europe. One of them was Andy Jablonski, a close friend of the family and a burly, energetic type who was about to be married. Andy became a paratrooper. My brothers and I knew him as a special friend. Another individual from our church, Bill Tellhorster, the oldest of eight children and the only son, became an infantryman.

D-Day, June 6, 1944, was a big event for just about everyone in the country—a do or die event for the outcome of the war. The bad news of thousands of deaths and injuries arrived rather quickly. But the invasion was heralded as a great victory.

Andy and Bill were both killed in the invasion. The invasion was a promising and sad event for our family, our friends, and our church. This was only one of the many similar stories for so many people throughout the war.

My family was mainly of German descent. Two great-aunts and their families still lived in Germany during World War II. We as children were taught to pray for their safety. Yet it was the US military that was trying to kill them. Families fighting and killing each other made no sense to me even at that young age. Yet it is characteristic of many wars. This senselessness of brothers fighting brothers was especially frequent in our own Civil War.

My twin cousins were drafted as well and sent to fight in Germany. Both returned home safely. One of them, Pfc. Arthur P. Kaufman, was captured. Toward the end of his confinement he was threatened with execution before being rescued by invading Soviet troops at the end of the war. He kept a diary from the day he was captured on Dec. 22, 1944 until his release on May 23, 1945—two weeks after V-E Day. Although he described rough conditions, he was treated reasonably well. For instance, shortly before his release, he was hospitalized and treated for dysentery by a doctor and given medication. Reviewing this incident caused me to think about "prisoners of war" these last 25 years of nearly constant wars in the Middle East and Afghanistan. Essentially, there have been no prisoners taken. As the Iraqi forces marched home at the end of the Persian Gulf War, many were indiscriminately killed by our pilots. "Take no prisoners" must have been the orders given. Individuals incarcerated and even tortured at Guantanamo and other detention sites operated by or in cooperation with the US purposely were not termed prisoners of war. That classification would have invited the rules of the Geneva Convention to be followed, with torturing prohibited.

In 1961, as an intern at the Henry Ford Hospital, I worked with a German doctor about my age. I couldn't help but think to myself: "Just a few years ago his relatives and mine were trying to kill each other—because their governments told them to do so. And today we're in medical training together learning how to save lives—what an irony!" I thought to myself, "War is such a waste!" It made no sense to me then; nor does it today.

As a child I was not aware of the deliberate US choice to saturation bomb cities including Dresden and Hamburg while ignoring the many efforts through international agreements to prevent targeting civilians. The Dresden bombing occurred in February of 1945 when the impending defeat of Germany was clear. One justification for the bombing was to send a message of our strength and determination to our "ally" the Soviet Union, setting the stage for the Cold War.

Propaganda is war's ally

My grandmother—who remembered discrimination against German-Americans during World War I—once explained to me that the German people didn't want the war. It was the government and the politicians who wanted the war, she said. This is generally true for most people around the world. It is why war propaganda is so necessary to generate support or, at least, tolerance for wars.

I never heard during World War II any discussion of the inadvisability of the war. Pearl Harbor silenced the war dissenters and the America First movement. The demand for superpatriotism under the conditions of all-out war meant that the debate was over with the attack on Pearl Harbor by the Japanese. It took decades for any real discussion to emerge regarding how President Franklin D. Roosevelt maneuvered us into a war he longed to be involved in, just as President Woodrow Wilson did for World War I.

Even today, authors who claim correctly, as Patrick Buchanan does in his book *Churchill, Hitler, and the Unnecessary War*, that both World War I and World War II were "unnecessary wars" are shunned and ridiculed. Such a suggestion is so at odds with how history is taught in most US schools that many people are unwilling to even consider arguments backing Buchanan's conclusion. We should not expect our government schools to provide an unbiased study and a full understanding of our involvement in foreign wars. But that will come as alternatives to government schools, with their federal government controls, develop. Homeschoolers will tend to receive a much more enlightened and accurate history of our foolish foreign entanglements.

As a child during World War II it was hard not to hear constant news about the war's progress. My Dad regularly tuned in to hear Lowell Thomas and Gabriel Heatter for the government slant on the war. Movie theaters always played a newscast with visuals to dramatize the ongoing war. Newspapers of course were important for gleaning what was going on. Those were the vehicles for keeping up with the various battles and war plans we were permitted to hear about. They were also used to prop up support for the war effort. TVs were uncommon, and my family did not have one. There was no internet. There were three major radio networks and mostly submissive large newspapers.

War hurts the economy

Life during the war, as I recall, was mostly austere. It was a continuation of the Great Depression.

Those who argue, typically for self-serving reasons, that the Great Depression ended because of our entering the war are wrong. They perpetrate an economic theory that is dangerous even today. We still frequently hear that war is a possible "solution" to our weak economy. Building drones and bombs, blowing things up, killing people, and generating hatred toward us is a no-brainer solution, they suggest, because in war the GDP rises and we all feel better. But, in reality, the country grows poorer, the standard of living goes down, and price inflation worsens. War also carries the dread and despair brought by actual and feared death, injury, and destruction. But, war profiteers don't complain. The interventionists will use any excuse to foment wars, including deeply flawed arguments for why war is healthy for the economy.

Even though quite young, I remember rationing and the government issued stamps that were required to buy meat, gasoline, butter, and many other products. And to no one's surprise black markets sprung up. Even my dad, who was as straitlaced as any patriotic American, bought meat for our family on the black market, i.e., the free market.

Being in the dairy business, we had to collect ration stamps when we sold butter. My brothers and I participated in this government rationing program when we dealt with customers at our home dairy and while out on home delivery.

No one questioned the rationing program. Everyone was told how it would help win the war. The war drove every decision. It was not until much later, with the study of Austrian economics, that I came to understand that rationing is the worst thing to do to prevent, or deal with, shortages. The more scarce the resources and goods to be distributed, the greater the need for market allocation.

With wage and price controls, which were in place during the war, it should have been expected that rationing would follow. Price controls always lead to shortages and rationing. The mess, created by the government, cries out for a free market solution. That solution is the black market. It's called a "black" market just to disparage it because it illegally challenges the government-controlled market.

During this period when the auto industry had been converted to making tanks and planes, I remember only one new automobile in our town. The car was sold under special allocation to one of the two MDs living in our town. It was a 1943 Pontiac. I remember the car being discussed, especially since after a year it was considered trash. The cars of the late 1930s and early '40s—before the attack on Pearl Harbor—were considered much better and functioned quite well until owners replaced them during the economic growth that finally came after the war ended.

My mother frequently delivered news to my dad as he worked in the dairy, which was in the basement of our home. They both were obviously opposed to the horrors of war, but my mother more often expressed her disdain for war. She had a great desire for the war to end.I know exactly where I was on July 16, 1945. I was assisting my dad in the milk bottling process in our basement. My mother, after hearing on the radio about the news of the first atomic bomb being exploded in Alamogordo, New Mexico, rushed to tell my dad with great excitement. The excitement came of course because it was now everyone's opinion that the war would soon end. Victory in Europe, V-E Day, had already been accomplished on May 8, 1945.

Little did my mother, or almost anyone else at the time, know how unnecessary it was to quickly follow through with the use of nuclear weapons on both Hiroshima and Nagasaki.

The "bomb" was successfully tested on July 16, 1945. Just 21 days later, on August 6, Hiroshima was bombed. Nagasaki was bombed three days later on August 9.

The official end to the war came on V-J Day, September 2, 1945. The celebrations were exciting and memorable for me as a 10-year-old who did not remember any time without war talk and austerity.

Franklin D. Roosevelt and the illusion of political parties

Up until April 12, 1945 Franklin D. Roosevelt was the only president of whom I had any memory.

When Roosevelt's death was announced, I cheered. Not that I had much of an opinion, but he must not have been very popular in the Paul household. My dad reprimanded me for expressing pleasure at the president's death. My dad explained to me that it is wrong to cheer someone's death even if you do not endorse what he had done.

My parents' disapproval of FDR had little to do with the strong disapproval I now have for his policies. His devotion to welfare, big government, and the Federal Reserve, along with his desire to get us into the war despite his campaign promises of 1940, are my complaints. As a candidate Roosevelt constantly repeated his pledge to stay out of the war. For example, on October 30, 1940 in Boston, he declared, "I have said this before, but I shall say it again and again and again: Your boys are not going to be sent into any foreign wars." Saying this while all the while secretly conspiring to enter the war at the right moment does not command respect.

I do remember the 1940 election, with Wendell Willkie the Republican nominee in opposition to FDR. The election results were met with disappointment in our household simply because a Democrat defeated a Republican. That elections often amount to a pretense of a contest between two individuals actually cut from the same cloth is something that has only recently been emphasized and is still not believed by many.

I was brought up believing Democrats in Congress sabotaged all President Herbert Hoover's efforts to end the Great Depression and that this caused the depression's prolongation. Democrats were bad; Republicans were good. Murray Rothbard, in his book *America's Great Depression*, finally explained to me the real culprit: the Federal Reserve's easy credit system and the policies the Fed pursued in the 1920s. Hoover and FDR's economic policies were close to being the same regardless of their differing rhetoric and promises. Likewise there probably wouldn't have been any major difference between a Willkie presidency and another four years with FDR. But a lot of people then believed, as many people still do today, that the Republicans and the Democrats offer real differences in policy. Both political parties in the 1930s and '40s, as today, endorsed foreign intervention, corporate subsidies, welfare for the poor, and a flexible interpretation of the Constitution. Both parties, for the last hundred years, have also supported the income tax and the Federal Reserve System.

In addition to maneuvering us into war, Roosevelt advanced the evil prolongation of the war. FDR's mantra was that nothing less than "unconditional surrender" would do. This phrase was constantly repeated, whipping up a frenzy so strong that people cheered the obliteration of Hiroshima and Nagasaki. I heard the "unconditional surrender" language constantly in the news and in the public schools I attended.

The justification has always been that the destruction of these two cities, along with the killing of people in the cities, prevented the many deaths and injuries of American troops that would have otherwise occurred in an invasion of Japan.

The real story is much different. Japan was already defeated and was on the verge of surrendering. With a little patience and common sense we could have wound down the war without the cataclysmic bombing of Hiroshima and Nagasaki. Besides, even after the nuclear attack, the US permitted Hirohito to retain his status as emperor.

No time back then or since has there been much discussion of the significance of Roosevelt's executive order on July 26, 1941 that froze all Japanese assets in the US. This occurred four months before Pearl Harbor. It essentially created an oil embargo on the Japanese. Such sanctions are a deeply flawed policy that we continue to use today, to our detriment.

I brought up the executive order in a US House of Representatives Foreign Affairs Committee discussion to warn of unintended consequences that might present themselves once sanctions were placed on Iran, as so many unintended consequences have occurred as a consequence of such a policy throughout history. My comment was promptly ridiculed by another committee member who revealed he had either never heard about the significance of the oil embargo on Japan or just wanted to hear nothing of it. Similarly, many people will shut down any discussion of how tariffs the US government imposed on the South had something to do with the Civil War. Even today the war propaganda of decades past prevents people from learning from history.

An explanation that Japan attacked in reaction to our punishing sanctions was of no interest to anyone after Pearl Harbor, and understandably so. Sorting out emotions from facts under these conditions is impossible—just as it was after the more recent 9/11 attack. Cooler heads never prevail under these circumstances. It's always just hoped that the historians will expose the truth to prevent future tragic errors.

Neoconservatives have written about "getting lucky" with a "Pearl Harbor event." Michael Ledeen wrote for example in his 1999 book *Machiavelli on Modern Leadership*: "Of course, we can always get lucky. Stunning events from outside can providently awaken the enterprise from its growing torpor, and demonstrate the need for renewal, as the devastating Japanese attack on Pearl Harbor in 1941 so effectively aroused the United States from its soothing dreams of permanent neutrality...." Then the 9/11 attack aroused war fever against Muslims and Arabs in the Middle East. This is precisely the reason that "false flags" are popular tools for those who see war as noble and heroic in their effort to promote an agenda that is never noble but always self-serving. And there's nothing heroic about chickenhawks, of which there are many.

The aspiration to end war, the reality of perpetual war

Even at the age of 10, when World War II ended, I was quite certain that war should be avoided if at all possible. I knew then that I dreaded the possibility of taking up arms and killing people. Descriptions of concentration camps and torture terrified me. I prayed that neither I nor any other human being would ever have to suffer that way again.

In my college days, as the Korean War was winding down, my optimism about ending war and killing decreased. I instead assumed that I, like so many others, would one day be drafted. This helped prompt my decision to go to medical school. I knew that I wanted no part of the killing and believed that being in a position to save lives was more to my liking.

On June 5, 1950, less than five years after V-J Day (September 2, 1945), I heard my mother express her deep concern about the breakout of yet another war: this time in Korea. In consternation she wondered, "How can the people accept yet another war so soon." At that time she was 42 years old and remembered World War I and the horrors of World War II that so recently ended. She did not ask "Why?" She asked just "How?"

Though I heard expressions many times about the sadness of another war, I never heard it expressed that we entered the Korean War without a congressional declaration of war. I do recall a teacher about that time praising—maybe it was just wishful thinking—the benefits of the United Nations and how it would keep the peace. It was on June 27, 1950 that the Security Council authorized its first "peace" keeping mission. It turns out that the United Nations was to orchestrate a war, the opposite of keeping peace. Very few at that time thought about or realized how the process for the US to engage in war was being forever changed. No more need for congressional approval. Consent would come merely from UN resolutions, NATO authority, or presidential executive orders for the foreseeable future

Perpetual global war would not come until the new century arrived. Lies by our leaders overcame the natural resistance of the people who had largely settled into apathy, ignorance, and denial regarding foreign policy. US foreign policy is now far from the restraints in the Constitution and the advice of our Founders in their effort to keep us out of war. With the executive branch acting along with cooperation of international organizations, the inordinate power of the "king" to go to war has been restored to our modern-day president.

By the time the Korean "police action"—not a war since only Congress can declare war—broke out I was a freshman in high school. Shortly thereafter, one of our coaches, who had served in World War II, was redrafted. Not too long afterwards we received the sad news of his death in Korea. My response was, "Why does this have to happen? It makes no sense." Though I was completely unaware of the politics, the lack of any national security threat, and the war's illegality, the war seemed wrong to me.

Though a few politicians at the time, including Senator Robert Taft, raised serious questions regarding the war, I never heard any discussion of the pros and cons of going to war. Indeed, even though there was no dramatic event like an attack on Pearl Harbor to unite the people, any objection would have been considered unpatriotic and not supportive of the troops. There had long been this admonition, as there is today, that foreign policy and fighting foreign wars must be bipartisan with the people unified, that is, with no dissent—at least at the beginning of the war.

I am optimistic that today that attitude is changing for the better. The majority of the American people opposed military action against Syria in the latter half of 2013. Still, there is much tolerance of our constant smaller wars as many people just pretend the wars don't exist. There's no real endorsement, but also no real objection. Drone warfare is more sterile. It's neat—no infantry involvement and thus fewer American casualties. Staring one's victims in their eyes as they die is discomforting. Thinking about casualties is unsettling. Many people, with other pressing concerns, find it best to slip into denial. Capital punishment to make it more tolerable is a medical IV to put the criminal to "sleep." No more public square hangings, firing squads, or guillotines. Certainly no one wants to witness collateral damage while "terrorists" defend their homeland from invaders from faraway places. Who wants to be tormented by seeing children and women die at funerals and weddings at our hands? Closing one's eyes to the destruction is easier than dealing with the reality of "preemptive" war and its ugly consequences.

This tolerance of war and the policies driven by the special interests allow for the constant wars with little outrage expressed. This has to change if we are to live in a more peaceful world.

What to like and not like about Ike

The 1952 election was all about war. I remember the speeches, but I was still too young to vote. I was intrigued by Ike's promise to go to Korea if he was elected.

I did vote on a real paper ballot however four years earlier in a mock election with my 19 classmates in the eighth grade. The vote was 19 to 1 in favor of Thomas Dewey, the Republican nominee. It was a Republican community. I was fascinated to hear Harry Truman pound away at "the do-nothing Congress," though I knew little about any other issue. I never told my parents that I voted for Truman. But, even then, a Republican victory would have changed little.

Ike did go to Korea. No nukes were dropped, which many people feared would happen. President Dwight D. Eisenhower had his shortcomings, but he said there was no need for the atomic bombs to have been dropped on Hiroshima and Nagasaki. A decent person from the military should always drift toward an antiwar position. General Smedley Butler's 1935 book *War is a Racket* is a classic condemnation of war.

Even with Ike's flaws, he's credited with ending the Korean War as he promised. Of course our involvement in the war should have never happened in the first place.

From 1953 to 1961, though the Marines were used under Eisenhower on a few occasions, no major military conflict began during his presidency. According to new revelations by Stephen Kinzer in his 2013 book *The Brothers*, though Eisenhower had a reputation for avoiding war per se, he was very involved in multiple covert wars. One thing is for sure: Eisenhower was not much of a noninterventionist. Ike supported and encouraged Secretary of State John Foster Dulles and CIA Director Allen Dulles in many actions around the world from which we continue to suffer blowback and unintended consequences. Many people know about the overthrowing of Iranian elected leader Mohammad Mosaddegh, but the Dulles brothers along with Eisenhower also supported covert activity in Vietnam, Cuba, the Middle East, Central America, and elsewhere. Some of these interventions were considered "successful," others failures. But, they all planted the seeds of resentment that persist today and will continue to undermine our national and financial security.

A student demonstration in Budapest in 1956 ignited the Hungarian Revolution. It lasted just over two weeks and was crushed by the invasion of Soviet tanks. I recall talk of the US getting involved, but Eisenhower quickly squelched that idea. He was harshly criticized by the "hawks" of that era for not sending military support to the revolutionaries.

The Hungarian Revolution didn't catch my attention as

much as the October of 1956 Israeli, French, and British attack on Egypt. This was a reaction to Egyptian President Gamal Abdel Nasser nationalizing the Suez Canal in July of 1956. A student at Gettysburg College at that time, I was keenly aware of the draft. I heard the news while working out in the pool as a member of the swimming team, and I remember thinking rather decidedly that if war came I would be drafted and taken out of school.

Eisenhower quickly objected to entering the conflict and patiently worked for a negotiated settlement—to my delight. Other than that, I did not think much about politics during my college days. I was not so much excited about Eisenhower's foreign policy as I was happy I was off the hook for being drafted.

The agreement Eisenhower negotiated required Britain and France to end military action and Israel to withdraw from Sinai, impressively with support from the Soviet Union in spite of the fact that there was an ongoing crisis with the US and Russia at that time over Hungary.

The concern I had for a few days in October of 1956 was the high point of my concern or thoughts about politics per se and foreign policy in particular during my college years. I was much more into pre-med studies and participation in sports.

The draft didn't reach me until six years later when I was a medical resident at the Henry Ford Hospital in Detroit in the heat of the Cuban missile crisis. Also at that time, US military involvement in Vietnam was expanding. From then on, personal experience and observation intensified my interest in the nature of foreign policy and how mistakes and deception lead to unnecessary wars.

I certainly didn't have an understanding of how and why our presidents directed foreign policy as they did. My doubts were building and questions were growing in my mind, but

I never heard addressed in any public discussion or broached by any college professor the subject of the noninterventionist foreign policy that the Founders had advocated.

The atmosphere with the Cold War in the 1950s made it difficult even to suggest that the US wasn't destined to be in charge of a world empire. Today it's gratifying that millions of people, especially college-age people, are keenly aware of what a noninterventionist foreign policy is all about. The failure of neoconservatism in foreign affairs can no longer be hidden from view. Yet, we have a long way to go to win over those in high places who appear destined to push the US Empire into national bankruptcy. That bankruptcy, though, would soon make unaffordable their pursuit of world domination, especially as that pursuit also becomes less tolerated by a world fed up with US invasions, occupations, and constant spying.

I was no hero in the Air Force

It wasn't long before another war forced me to continue to develop my position on war.

By the time I was sworn in to the Air Force, the Cuban missile crisis was over. I had been informed by Selective Service that I would be put in the Army as a buck private unless I wanted to "volunteer." If I volunteered I could pick my branch of service and maybe where I'd be stationed. Also, I would be given an officer rank, and I could practice medicine. I decided on becoming an Air Force flight surgeon. As with the millions before me, I became the "universal soldier" described in Buffy Sainte-Marie's song.

I had strong suspicions at the time that the war was wrong, though I did not yet fully understand the great evil of our policy of endless, undeclared wars. There were only a few draftees at the time—in the early '60s—resisting the war. Large-scale resistance came later with the senseless carnage that occurred after President Johnson's 1965 escalation orchestrated by Defense Secretary Robert McNamara. Though annoyed that my medical training had been interrupted, I never contemplated taking on the US government on a point of principle.

My active duty in the Air Force and the Air National Guard ran from 1963 to 1968—two and half years in San Antonio, Texas and two and a half years in Pittsburgh, Pennsylvania.

Today it annoys me to no end when a chickenhawk thanks me for my service as if I were some sort of hero. Merely wearing a military uniform doesn't qualify anyone as a hero. Those encounters occur rarely for me for a reason. If it's discovered that a former military member is not supportive of preemptive war or is even willing just to question it, he is then considered unpatriotic by the prowar crowd.

Look at the way John Kerry and Chuck Hagel were treated during Senate hearings regarding their nominations for, respectively, secretary of state and secretary of defense. Both were accused of being "weak on the military" because at one time in their lives they challenged the wisdom of carelessly waging war. They weren't even close to being noninterventionist, but the radical chickenhawks wanted to discredit them for their less-than-hawkish statements. Kerry and Hagel's appointments were not stopped, and many progressives welcomed their appointments. It turned out that, when Kerry and Hagel supported a hawkish position of the president, they served to neutralize criticism by those who supported their appointments over more hawkish candidates. The two Cabinet members were probably meant to give President Obama some cover for his military aggressiveness overseas.

During my time in the Air Force I certainly was no hero. Though I now espouse strong antiwar opinions, I then did nothing to resist war. But that's why the young are taken to fight nonsensical wars—being less confident in their beliefs and having less ability to speak out and resist. Besides, who at the age of 18 or 28 wants to be labeled un-American and un-patriotic? Who at that age wants to become a lawbreaker and jeopardize his future career? Yet a few did.

One thing for sure, Muhammad Ali stood his ground and refused to go thousands of miles from home to kill people who never did him any harm—a heroic stand. For this stand, he, like others, was arrested and faced imprisonment. What the government wants is efficient, sterile killers in immoral wars who can be awarded medals and paraded before cheering audiences as great patriotic defenders of our liberty.

I traveled as part of my duty as a flight surgeon, though I never went to Vietnam. I earned a private pilot's license during this time.

Part of the duty required that I perform physical examinations on warrant officers anxious to obtain flying status and train to fly helicopters. Most of them couldn't wait to enter battle in Vietnam. I often wondered later how many never came home since so many helicopters were shot down and the pilots killed.

On November 21, 1963, I was the medical officer in charge at Kelly Air Force Base near San Antonio. There was a tremendous amount of excitement as President Kennedy visited briefly. It turned out that there was no need for me to be directly involved since his visit at Kelly went uneventfully. The next day in Dallas was quite different.

Later on, while in the Air National Guard, I performed many physicals on inductees—individuals drafted to fight in the infantry. We can be certain that many of them were killed in the war. What kind of heroic service was I performing? It is true that my refusal would not have changed the course of the war. The only thing that achieved that was the demonstrations by Americans at home against the stupid foreign policy that led to nearly 60,000 Americans being killed before we admitted we lost the war and realized that we should never have been involved in it. Public opinion is a powerful tool, if not the ultimate tool, for changing policies of the seemingly omnipotent political leaders. The greatest danger is an apathy that allows for evil to thrive when bad people rule over us and provoke nationalistic and patriotic fervor that intimidates many into compliance.

Robert McNamara, as secretary of defense, was a major force behind our foolish escalation in the 1960s. In his memoir *In Retrospect: The Tragedy and Lessons of Vietnam* McNamara more or less confessed that serious mistakes were made. When Terry Gross asked McNamara in a 1995 National Public Radio interview "Do you think an apology is appropriate?" McNamara responded as follows: "Well, if you want me to apologize, of course. But that's not the issue. The issue isn't apology. You don't, I'll call it, correct a wrong by apologizing. You can correct a wrong only if you understand how it occurred and you take steps to ensure it won't happen again."

A heartwrenching incident was the death of a neighbor's only son, who was serving in Vietnam. I was still in the Air National Guard at the time. Visiting the family at the funeral home was indeed sad. The son had finished law school, and the plan was that as soon as he returned from Vietnam he would join his dad's law practice. All I could do was shed a tear and think loudly to myself: "What a waste, and for what?"

Promoting peace, overcoming the war propagandists

Knowledge of those friends and neighbors who died in war, in combination with a growing understanding of how and why most wars are fought, played a significant role in building my determination to advocate for a noninterventionist foreign policy.

Though the several deaths in World War II, Korea, and Vietnam I was aware of may seem small in number, they led me to consider the tragic losses and consequential suffering that families endure on all sides of every war. Especially difficult was coming to an understanding that war almost always is based on lies by one's own government and has nothing to do with ensuring national security, protecting liberty, or defending the Constitution.

Though history and the special interests benefiting from wars may suggest that noninterventionism cannot be implemented, there's no reason to assume that an effort to diminish the probability of war will fail. To not make the effort automatically concedes too much authority to the politicians.

My indirect exposure to war for most of my life constantly pushed me toward seeking, and becoming comfortable with, a pro-peace philosophy, as well as refusing to be intimidated by the false charges that such a position is unpatriotic, un-American, and expresses a lack of concern for military personnel. Neither does a pro-peace philosophy represent a callous disregard for one's natural desire to defend one's country from an actual attack. The professionals at war propaganda seem to always win this argument, but, with the ability today to spread information through alternative methods, we can diminish the power and influence of the war propagandists.

I found the full answer to explain and defend a noninterventionist foreign policy by discovering many authors who wrote about the issue and had a good understanding of international politics. The more I learned about how the system worked, the more convinced I became that war is rarely justified, i.e., defensive in nature. I found that almost always governments lie and use war propaganda to incite enough hatred to cause young soldiers to accept traveling many miles to kill strangers who never committed an act of aggression against them or their country.

It still amazes me how complicit the media are in propagandizing for war. This is true whether it's a Republican or Democratic-leaning entity. Both sides spout the lies delivered by government officials to encourage public support for wars. Whether the president is a Republican or a Democrat, the media will be supportive. It just may be that the owners of the large media entities are closely connected to the military-industrial complex.

Our economic policy, and in particular the Federal Reserve, is intertwined in global finance and our foreign policy. Without the power over the creation of money and credit employed by the politicians and central bankers working in secret, most wars could not be fought. The people would never tolerate the taxation and borrowing required to pay for the wars. Inflating the currency is more convenient and less noticeable. To the benefit of those who promote war, the cost of war is hidden and the payment delayed.

When I first went to Congress, I was strongly opposed to intervention in the affairs of other nations, and I strongly defended all true free trade efforts as my early speeches indicate. Yet I became even more convinced about the virtue of nonaggression over the years. Meanwhile, the Washington establishment, both Republican and Democrat, increasingly promoted a militaristic and interventionist foreign policy, especially after 9/11.

After the fall of the Soviet Union, support grew for the US to become the world policeman, and many claimed that we had a moral obligation to do so because of our "exceptionalism." We had the authority to act, it was asserted, as the final arbitrator of all world conflicts.

The more the US did overseas, the greater became my resentment and fear of the unintended consequences that were bound to come.

The dollars spent on the military and how they contribute to our bankruptcy is of no concern to the politicians. War profiteering in the US has run rampant. Most Republicans and many Democrats see military spending as a Holy Grail that cannot be challenged.

In spite of this nearly universal support by our political leaders of both parties, resentment of this deeply flawed policy has become more prevalent, especially on university campuses. The dollars spent, the growing debt, the weak economy, the illegality of the wars, the trampling of liberty as a consequence of continual war, and student debt without job opportunities are aspects of a situation that has not been well received by students on American campuses.

All of this has led to resentment of and disgust for the waste of war. If encouraged, this resentment and disgust can grow and become a significant factor promoting changing the attitude that dominates Washington, DC.

The dangers to our liberty, peace, and prosperity have increased manifold since 2001. This has only encouraged me more to speak out and do whatever I can to encourage others, in and out of politics, to question the rationales of US policies against which the Founders of this country were so strongly opposed.

It appears that common sense is not about to break out in our nation's capital. Whether it's the irrationality of our foreign policy or our domestic welfare state, it looks like these problems will continue and will only end when the US government's credit runs out. In the meantime, gaining allies in support of a noninterventionist foreign policy and nonaggression will be vital to rebuilding a free society. To succeed, an enlightened understanding of government limits and the nature of war is required.

Remember boy that your forefathers died
Lost in millions for a country's pride
They never mention the trenches of Belgium
When they stopped fighting and they were one

A spirit stronger than war was working that night
December 1914 cold, clear and bright
Countries' borders were right out of sight
They joined together and decided not to fight

"All Together Now" The Farm

2

Our Peaceful Nature

Is peace more natural for mankind than war? It has been said that it is not in man's nature to seek war. If that is the case, why have so many wars been fought throughout history? It probably can be explained by the good versus evil character of man. But I don't believe wars are inevitably compelled by our natural instincts and that the only thing left to do is pick sides. Though evil people will forever be with us, they are greatly outnumbered by those who are repulsed by the systematic slaughter of innocent victims in senseless wars promoted by the few.

Allowing the war-prone individuals, bent on evil, to gain power in governments must be one of the most significant reasons that wars erupt. Individuals with prowar inclinations are naturally aggressive and seek power over others. As Friedrich Hayek argued in his book *The Road to Serfdom*, "the worst get on top." The power seekers also convince themselves that they are superior to average people and have a moral responsibility to use force to mold the world as they see fit. The propaganda is that war is for the sake of "goodness and righteousness." Isabel Paterson described it in her book *The God of the Machine* as "the humanitarian with a guillotine." Those who are more prone to peace tend to be complacent and to not resist the propaganda required to mobilize otherwise peaceful people to fight and die for the lies told and the false noble goals proposed by the self-appointed moral leaders.

The Christmas truce

One well-known war versus peace story vividly portrays the conflict inherent in men wanting peace being required to fight by men who want war. The incident occurred on December 24, 1914 on the front lines near the beginning of World War I. British, French, and Belgian troops and the facing German troops called a truce. The troops stopped the killing and together celebrated Christmas Eve.

This story of that most unusual Christmas Eve demonstrates the age-old conflict between man's natural peaceful inclinations and politicians' obsession with war.

That Christmas Eve's spontaneous cessation of fighting on the front lines was remarkable in that it was such a rare event. It just didn't make sense to the young men of Christian nations that they should spend Christmas Eve and Christmas Day slaughtering each other.

At quite a young age, when I first became aware of what Christianity was teaching, a thought crossed my mind: Two Christian nations should never have to go to war. I later learned that this was not the case historically, much to my disappointment. In World War I, people of Christian nations were fighting and killing each other, contradicting the message of peace that Christ taught. Today, however, it is often not so much that one Christian nation is fighting another as that hatred has developed between factions of Christianity and factions of Islam. I believe this is a distortion of both religions. Yet the individuals who advocate for war are adamant about the evil of the other side. Unfortunately, militarism has overwhelmed the many who throughout history have advocated spiritual and ethical support for a more peaceful world. The government propaganda has great influence on the complacent, and the temptation for conformity takes over.

World War I was only a few months old. The hate that automatically grows on both sides as the violence increases was not at a fever pitch on that very special and different Christmas Eve. That growth in hate came later, once it was clear that many of those soldiers on both sides who were involved in the truce that exceptional night were wrong in their belief that the war would end quickly. The dramatic and spontaneous truce that Christmas Eve spawned by the wishes of young German, British, French, and Belgian soldiers reveals the true nature of most human beings forced into wars that have no meaning.

This is why warfare, especially in the decades following World War I, involved government conditioning of soldiers to kill their fellow human beings. The enemy had to be dehumanized, and epithets were used to help— "krauts," "Japs," "gooks," etc.—lest people's natural instincts prevail. Without conditioning to kill, some soldiers, especially draftees, were found shooting above the target to avoid killing the enemy. Since World War II we've seen a concerted US military effort to eliminate any natural instincts against killing other than for true defense of one's homeland. This effort has become more necessary as our wars have become more offensive in nature.

This most unusual event on this particular Christmas Eve on the front lines of a brutal war was detested by the politicians and the military leaders who believed the truce had to be stopped. Peace could not be permitted to break out among troops who were supposed to kill and die in a war brought about by politicians hundreds of miles away.

My thought when I first read about the Christmas truce was: "What a difference it would make if soldiers could go on strike." In contrast, Buffy Sainte-Marie suggests in her song "Universal Soldier" that soldiers always blindly accept orders and never resist. But what if those who are required to do the killing on both sides refused to fight in a war that is not justified and makes no sense? That's what happened on that special Christmas Eve in 1914. For a brief period both sides refused to fight. Instead they preferred to sing Christmas carols, play soccer, exchange gifts including tobacco and alcohol, eat and drink together, and bury the dead.

It had been just five months since the beginning of an insane war in which 17 million people eventually would die, and in which hundreds of thousands had already been killed. Of the 17 million people killed, seven million were civilians. So much for a "humane" war or rules to protect noncombatants.

What a difference it would make if the power of political leaders to start wars was very restricted and if the soldiers would refuse to fight if wars were started nonetheless.

The Christmas truce ended when the soldiers on both sides were compelled, with threats, to resume the insane killing, which they did on December 26 and in some parts of the front days later.

The strange story of peace breaking out in the midst of a vicious war was preserved by letters sent home by many participants. The best collection of the details of that Christmas Eve was compiled by Stanley Weintraub in his stirring depiction of the event in his book *Silent Night*.

Weintraub reports of an interview with Carl Mühlegg 50

years after that special night. Mühlegg relates how he carried a small Christmas tree across no man's land, as guns were still firing, to initiate the truce. He explained that the machine gun fire did not deter him because, "[a]fter all, I was father Christmas bearing a decorated tree, although… with a gun over my shoulder and a bag of ammunition!" Upon completing his crossing, Mühlegg recounts, "I handed the captain the little Christmas tree."

The British captain lit the tree's candles and wished his soldiers, the German nation, and the whole world "peace according to the message from the angel." Later near midnight the guns grew quiet and the soldiers of the two armies mingled in the middle of no man's land between the armies' positions. Mühlegg, according to Weintraub, wrote of the event with passion: "Never was I as keenly aware of the insanity of war."

Just as my grandmother had explained to me when I was a child, the German people didn't want war.

Another profound recollection relating to that special Christmas truce, also recorded by Weintraub, occurred on March 31, 1930, 15 years after the event of 1914. A British House of Commons member in debate reflected on his participation in the Christmas truce. Sir H. Kingsley Wood said he "took part in what was well known at the time as a truce. We went over in front of the trenches and shook hands with many of our German enemies. A great number of people [now] think we did something that was degrading." He disagreed: "The fact is that we did it, and I then came to the conclusion that I have held very firmly ever since, that if we had been left to ourselves there would never have been another shot fired. For a fortnight the truce went on. We were on the most friendly terms, and it was only the fact that we were being controlled by others that made it necessary for us to start trying to shoot one another again." Not to my surprise he knew exactly where the problem lay. He said it was "the grip of a political system which was bad, and I and others who were there at the time determined there and then never to rest ... until we had seen whether we could change it."

I'm sure countless others, forced to fight in wars over the ages, felt the same way. But propaganda, fear, and threats of being accused of being unpatriotic and treasonous are powerful means of controlling the young soldiers who are told their fighting is crucial for the country's survival. It's the young soldiers who must risk and even lose their lives. It's the typical politicians, who have been around for thousands of years, who have continued the carnage with their humanitarian lies and demands for wars.

A later ballad "Christmas in the Trenches," written by John McCutcheon about the uselessness of war, and probably related to the 1914 Christmas truce, concludes:

> *The ones who call the shots won't be among the dead and lame,*
> *And on each end of the rifle we are the same.*

In mentioning another spontaneous truce—during the Siege of Tobruk in Libya during World War II—Weintraub relates a soldier's comment: "Nobody said we couldn't like them, they just said we had to kill them. All a bit stupid, isn't it?" Obviously it is stupid, and it's also stupid to cling to this notion that the frequency of wars cannot be greatly reduced. To say that the wars and constant killing are destined to last forever is like saying long ago that people would only walk forever because the wheel had not yet been and never would be invented.By the end of World War I there were thousands of courts-martial for not fighting. Some were killed on the spot by their superiors. For others sentences, including death sentences, were issued. Soldiers of all armies, especially near the end of the war, just refused to fight. Deserting or refusing to fight is considered treasonous. Yet, it may be this act that requires the greatest courage.

Shortly after the guns of World War I were silenced, the seeds were sown in the Treaty of Versailles for yet another even greater human tragedy—World War II. Training and conditioning soldiers to kill and never fraternize with the enemy sought to ensure that a spontaneous truce would not occur in spite of the insanity of the killing in World War II, the Korean War, the Vietnam War, and other wars.

After World War I the League of Nations was established. The United Nations, created after World War II, replaced the League of Nations, with a mission supposedly to bring peace to the world. Yet, one of the UN's early major decisions on the subject was to expand the Korean civil war, resulting in approximately three million deaths of which two million were Korean civilians. Over 35,000 Americans lost their lives in this UN "police action," as Truman described it.

When the Christmas truce ended after Christmas Day in 1914, the promoters of hate won. Poison gas was used, and all the other insanities of war proceeded. Troops, whose instincts were to settle this dispute with songs and soccer games, soon were convinced that the enemy was less than human and that the slaughter had to go on. The carnage became worse. Twenty-seven months later, when the war was still stalemated, the US Congress declared war against Germany upon the urging of President Woodrow Wilson who had promised in his 1916 presidential campaign that the US would stay out of this war.

War propaganda, lies, and fears produced a patriotic, jingoistic response from the American people in support of sending over 100,000 Americans off to their death in the first major war of a century of wars for the United States—all in the name of patriotism and heroism!

Certainly up until now there is no evidence that war is becoming either less frequent or less horrendous.

Moments of compassion among World War II fighting

In almost all wars there are stories of combatants treating the enemy with compassion and a sense of humanity. It occurred in the American Civil War rather frequently.

A story Paul Chappell tells in his book *Peaceful Revolution* supports my contention that most people, including soldiers, prefer peace.

Captain Jack Tueller, one evening two weeks after D-Day, took his trumpet out to play. His commander advised him not to play since one German sniper remained uncaptured from the day's battle. Tueller thought that the German sniper was scared and lonely just as he was. Tueller played the German song "Lili Marleen." The next day, the German sniper surrendered to the Americans. Before being sent to a prison in England, he asked to meet the trumpet player. When they did meet the German soldier broke into tears and said: "When I heard that number that you played I thought about my fiancée in Germany. I thought about my mother and dad and about my brothers and sisters, and I could not fire." "He stuck out his hand and I shook the hand of the enemy. He was no enemy. He was scared and lonely like me," Tueller recounts.

It is these instincts—supported by reason—that governments are compelled to counter or there would be no one left to fight the old politicians' senseless wars. These instincts favoring peace are good and natural. The enthusiasm for needless war is evil and unnatural. The worst offenders are those who are unable to empathize with a dehumanized enemy. Fortunately, they are greatly outnumbered. Unfortunately, most societies allow the proponents of war to gain political power. And those who seek power with promises of peace often are either liars or succumb to the temptation to use brute force in dealing with other nations at the urging of the various special interests. The people, including those asked to fight, must resist the propagandists who promote war. Further, the people must insist on protecting the natural human desire for peace and liberty. It looks like it will take a philosophic revolution and a great deal of determination to permit these instincts to thrive.

Another amazing incident occurred a few days before Christmas in 1943. A B-17 bomber was severely damaged over enemy territory in Germany. It was being flown by 21-year-old West Virginia farm boy Charlie Brown who was on his second combat mission, his first as a pilot. Half of his crew was either wounded or dead. Brown was trying to fly the plane back to England. All of a sudden a German Messerschmitt Bf 109 fighter was within three feet of the B-17's right wingtip. The German pilot, who was close enough to look into the eyes of the American pilot, did not fire. Instead he just nodded to the American pilot, pointed, and, before flying off, saluted Brown. The American plane was able to limp back and land safely in England.

This story was written up by Adam Makos in his best-selling book, *A Higher Call.*

Quite a few people over many years have tried to explain this phenomenon of two avowed enemies suddenly refusing to kill. Some have argued that they are following a "warrior's code." Governments are determined to dehumanize the enemy. Yet it is difficult for soldiers to forget their own humanity once they look into the eyes of the enemy they're directed to fight.

Human nature is such that when one person is about to take another's life it's best not to look into his eyes as he breathes his last. Even gangsters frequently execute their opponents with a bullet to the back of the head, as do some modern-day dictators. The Nazis, according to Paul Chappell in *Peaceful Revolution*, stopped using the firing squad to murder huge numbers of people at a time not for efficiency as some have argued, but instead because executioners pursuing the old way essentially went mad. I'm sure the use of the gas chambers didn't fully solve the problem. Only psychopaths can adapt to such cruelty.

The traditional warrior's code was intended to take a very violent act of killing another human being and make it acceptable. If only the fighters knew they were following a set of rules, as if they were participating in a soccer game, it might seem more humane.

Being chivalrous, in rare moments, is likely the best people can do in resisting their government's demand for the use of force in a war that they know deep down in their hearts makes no sense. Being noble for a few moments and sparing a life is an instinct of humanity shouting out in an attempt to preserve one's own sanity. Chivalry may be helpful, but in the long term it cannot erase the guilt associated with the fighting and killing in the many wars that do not serve the interest of the people.

The story about the B-17 bomber pilot and the pilot of the German Messerschmitt Bf-109 fighter did not end a few days before Christmas in 1943. The two met again 46 years later. Both men over the decades thought about the incident and wondered whether they would ever again find each other. After searching they finally met in 1990, and their families eventually got to know each other. That included a large number of Brown's family members who would have never been born if the German pilot had not looked into Brown's eyes and saw a terrified human being expecting immediately to breathe his last.

When the two men were reunited, one of the first questions Brown asked Franz Stigler, who had flown the German plane, was, "What were you pointing for?" Stigler explained that he was advising Brown to fly to Sweden since it was closer. But, it was Brown's first combat mission as a pilot, and he only knew his way back to England. No GPS back then!

The German pilot Franz Stigler and American pilot Charlie Brown became close friends and fishing buddies. The reunion was just as important to Stigler as it was to Brown because of the deep feelings associated with their encounter and a war they would have never started.

Both pilots were Christians. Stigler on that mission was carrying a rosary in his flight jacket. He passed his hand over the rosary as he made his decision not to pull the trigger. Firing would have certainly downed the B-17 and killed the still alive crew members. The American pilot, Lieutenant Brown, after he landed his plane and brought it to a stop in England, placed his hand over a Bible. Following this incident, both had to go back to the business of war and killing.

Stigler moved to Canada a few years after the war. Brown settled in Florida. Stigler said that his saving Brown's life was the only good thing that came out of the whole war for Stigler. Both men died in 2008 as close friends who were forced to face ugly realities of a ghastly war that need not have been.

Our leaders are hoping that, with modern-day warfare being fought remotely with cruise missiles, drones, and secret assassinations, the military personnel won't get hung up on the sentimentalities of looking in the eyes of those individuals about to die. But it's not going to work that way. If the drone operators refuse to look, which they frequently could do if they desired, they will still not be able to erase the consequences of their actions. Blowback will still come. Wedding parties and funerals are attacked, and the pictures from drone attacks make their way to the internet. The slain, frequently including women and children, will not be forgotten by the victims' families, nor by the operators of the weapons systems who will be reminded constantly of their acts as the retaliation continues. Truth will be haunting even if a remote war is fought and looking in the victims' eyes can be avoided.

When the wars of our nation did beckon,
A man barely twenty did answer the calling.
Proud of the trust that he placed in our nation,
He's gone,
But Eternity knows him, and it knows what we've done.

"The Grave" Don McLean

3

Opposing War in Congress

When I first ran for Congress in the 1974 general election my motivation for speaking out had more to do with monetary policy and the financial crisis that was ongoing as a consequence of the Nixon economic policies—especially the severing of the last link of gold to the dollar—than it did with foreign policy. US troops had been withdrawn from Vietnam, the draft had been discontinued, and the US was not participating in an active war.

Elected in 1976 to my first term in office and leaving Congress in 1985, foreign policy was not on the front burner for me. Although on entering Congress I firmly supported the noninterventionist foreign policy articulated by our early presidents and permitted by the Constitution, over the years I became much more firmly convinced that the policies of foreign intervention, endorsed by both political parties, would always cause a great deal of harm to us. I continued to read and study many both liberal and libertarian authors who over many years convinced me of the antiwar case and the benefits of minding our own business.

In that first tour in Congress, an attack that resulted in the death of 241 US military members in Beirut, Lebanon in 1983 prompted me to speak out against President Ronald Reagan's intervention in that nation. Reagan later in his memoirs expressed regret for his mistake and acknowledged that the troops would still be alive if he had only followed a policy of "neutrality."

Reagan wrote in his autobiography *An American Life*: "Perhaps we didn't appreciate fully enough the depth of the hatred and the complexity of the problems that make the Middle East such a jungle. Perhaps the idea of a suicide car bomber committing mass murder to gain instant entry to Paradise was so foreign to our own values and consciousness that it did not create in us the concern for the marines' safety that it should have. Perhaps we should have anticipated that members of the Lebanese military whom we were trying to assist would simply lay down their arms and refuse to fight their own countrymen. In any case, the sending of the marines to Beirut was the source of my greatest regret and my greatest sorrow as president."

While Reagan commented in his autobiography that, "in the weeks immediately after the bombing, I believed the last thing that we should do was to turn tail and leave," he concluded that "the irrationality of Middle Eastern politics forced us to rethink our policies there."

If Reagan and all the other presidents since could only have realized and acted in accord with the profoundness of this change of mind, the tragic, constant wars of the early part of the 21st century could have been averted. But, even Reagan, who was less hawkish than the two Bushes, Clinton, and

Obama, supported frequent and significant interventions.

On October 25, 1983, two days after the attack in Beirut, Reagan had the US military invade and "liberate" Grenada. Some called the invasion a distraction to chalk up a military victory. Other needless interventions under Reagan occurred as well: weapon sales to Iran and Iraq, illegal funding of the Nicaraguan Contras, aid to the Guatemalan military, support for the mujahideen of which Osama bin Laden was a part, and support for Jonas Savimbi's UNITA in Angola. The bombing of Libya in 1986 in an attempt to kill Muammar Gaddafi did not win us friends in the Arab world. And all this comes from the president less inclined to starting wars than all later presidents. Too bad the admonition of our early presidents to stay out of entangling alliances and the internal affairs of foreign nations and instead to offer trade and friendship to all nations has long been forgotten.

While no major ground war began under Reagan, the more limited interventions of his administration stirred my interest in foreign affairs. I believed that, instead of being forgotten, these interventions would contribute to resentment and cause blowback to be directed at us. So far the 21st century has confirmed my worst fears for retaliation. Tragically the aggressive nature of our foreign intervention only becomes worse. Too many believe that we're exceptional and that everyone around the world should love us even when we invade, kill, and undermine other nations' sovereignty.

Just as we can expect a cataclysmic end to a deeply flawed economic and monetary system, we should expect a similar end to the US Empire. And a strong case can be made that the two will reach their ends together.

My experiences before being elected to the House of Representatives helped encourage me to read those authors who wrote of the miscalculations for going to war. Though moving toward war is oftentimes deliberate, it is also often accomplished with gross miscalculations of the nature of the enemy and ignorance of the unintended consequences that might come, the duration and intensity of the war, the resulting carnage, and the economic costs. Almost always it seems that there are miscalculations as to the determination and plans of the opposition in any war. It's assumed by both sides that the other side will either back down or not be foolish enough to persist in fighting a no-win war.

During my years in office spanning constant conflicts in which we were involved at great financial and human cost, I continued to strengthen my belief that a noninterventionist foreign policy is a necessity for a free society to exist and thrive. It was easy to find experienced journalists and authors who made it clear that a drastically different foreign policy would prevent constant war.

With each year, starting with my first campaign in 1973-74 through leaving office in January of 2013, my conviction grew that most of our wars throughout our history should have been avoided. This firming of conviction occurred in spite of the superficial perception and so-called evidence that we have been fighting less traumatic wars since the Vietnam War ended in 1972.

Americans now seem less concerned about the tragedy of war since the military deaths are not listed in the tens of thousands. War injuries not resulting in death on the battlefield are a different matter and receive less attention than the number of American troops killed. The wounded and the mentally damaged sadly are neglected as we witness an epidemic of suicides of our veterans.

Unfortunately, complacency about war has grown among Americans as war appears to become more sterile. Drone warfare, which is endorsed by the most aggressive proponents of perpetual war, may limit our casualties. But the suffering of recipients of our launched missiles continues to cause hatred toward America to grow.

In the last 13 years, the wars in Iraq and Afghanistan, when compared to our two world wars, Korea, and Vietnam, have not resulted in staggering numbers of Americans killed. But the deaths of non-Americans as a consequence of our sanctions, invasions, and bombings are numbered in the hundreds of thousands. We may not be counting, but the Muslim world is. Recipients of such violence and their families have long memories.

We now live in an age of fourth-generation warfare. War is not fought for the most part as it has generally been fought over the years with one government's military fighting another government's military. Unofficial armies, sophisticated guerrilla warriors, and other groups have evolved in resisting foreign aggression, especially when their own governments pander too much to outside influence or the US tries to run the show, stir up civil strife, or affect elections.

Pretending to keep our hands clean by providing "secret" assistance to various warring factions and limiting our military involvement by using drones will not serve the cause of peace even if such actions are less noticeable and not condemned by the American people. The victims of this policy know exactly where the money and arms come from.

Though there have been fewer Americans killed in recent years than in the Korean and Vietnam Wars, my abhorrence of our involvement in foreign militarism has continued to grow. I see our militaristic foreign policy as immoral. It hurts our national security, profits special interests, and costs too much. It causes greater hatred toward and blowback on the American people. I see no upside to our "perpetual wars for perpetual peace." It's no longer a complaint about the "Ugly American."

Instead the "Ruthless American" is blaming others for acts of terrorism yet engaging constantly in the same.

When I returned to the House of Representatives in 1997, I asked to join the International Relations Committee, which has since been renamed the Foreign Affairs Committee, as well as to rejoin the Financial Services Committee since I had been on that committee (then called the Banking Committee) when in Congress between 1976 and 1985.

Requests of this sort go through one's state party delegation. In our Texas Republican delegation organizational meeting in January of 1997, those individuals representing the delegation on the Republican Steering Committee had an initially quite favorable response to my request. And at that time Texas had some clout since Texas had a 13-member Republican delegation. In 1976 I had become the fourth Republican member in the then much smaller Texas Republican delegation.

The Financial Services Committee was not considered a powerhouse committee at the time, though today it is. Having been on the committee before, I was assured it would be no problem to get back on. However, restoring my seniority on the committee—usually a routine process—was denied.

The weakest and least sought-after subcommittee was the Domestic Monetary Policy Subcommittee. This was the committee I had wanted to be on, and that wish was granted. It was my view that protecting the value of the currency is a high priority. Eventually I would spend two years as chairman of that subcommittee before leaving Congress, a position that afforded me a greater opportunity to quiz Federal Reserve Board Chairman Ben Bernanke and conduct monetary policy oversight hearings highlighting Austrian economics and sound money views.

The reasons for denying seniority for my earlier terms were easy to understand. Toeing the party line and giving up one's independence is necessary to advance through the system. It's called being a "team player," and it is something in which I had no interest. In December of 2012, shortly before I left the House of Representatives, Speaker John Boehner announced the removal of four House members from committees in the upcoming congressional term for the same reason. So, in some ways, just staying on the Financial Services Committee and ultimately becoming chairman of the Domestic Monetary Policy Subcommittee even for a short period of time was a bit of an achievement in a very corrupt political system.

The Foreign Affairs Committee was a different matter. When the Texas members of the Republican Steering Committee reported back, they said I'd be on the Financial Services Committee without seniority but no dice on the Foreign Affairs Committee. Initially they had told me with confidence that, with the Foreign Affairs Committee not a highly sought after committee, there would be no problem with me joining it. But, later, in a remarkably blunt statement my request was denied because, due to my opposition to foreign aid—to anyone, I was accused of not being a friend of Israel. I was pleased though that four years later, and without me changing my voting habits, I was, after persistent, polite requests, assigned to the Foreign Affairs Committee.

On the Foreign Affairs Committee I was in the middle of the debate on the crucial matters of war, and war in the Middle East and Afghanistan in particular. Nothing in this period made me the least bit sympathetic to the neocons' obsession with remaking the Middle East. Instead, I was motivated to counter all the war propaganda to which I had to listen.

Voting to authorize the use of force so George W. Bush could pursue those individuals who perpetrated the violence of 9/11 was the most difficult of all my votes. Though I was convinced that the attack was exactly what the CIA calls "blowback" for deeply flawed US policy in the Middle East and especially against Iraq, I could still not say we had no responsibility to deal with those responsible for 9/11 and to prevent another attack. I thought of the US foreign policy flaws that helped to bring about the Japanese attack on Pearl Harbor on December 7, 1941. But, after that attack, not to resist the Japanese was hardly an option.

The real crime, and it should have surprised no one, was the abuse of the authority given to President George W. Bush to deal with those responsible for 9/11. The president used the congressional authorization to pursue perpetual war anywhere in the world under the pretense that doing so was necessary for national security and related to the 9/11 attack. The tragedy is that we both never learn from the deeply flawed foreign policy and ignore the most beneficial action we could take—to change the foreign policy.

Even the president realized that the congressional authorization to pursue those involved in orchestrating events of 9/11 could not be stretched to justify a US military invasion and occupation of Iraq. The president worked diligently in 2002 to obtain additional authority from the United Nations and Congress to invade Iraq and never claimed that the invasion was authorized by the 2001 legislation. Later both Bush and Obama argued that the AUMF legislation, which approved the use of force in 2001, was open-ended and gave authority to pursue many of their military attacks as part of the Global War on Terror.

The invasion, war, and occupation to transform Afghanistan went far beyond the limited congressional authorization. These actions in Afghanistan were undertaken illegally without a declaration of war, just as the war in Iraq and many of other places since then have been undertaken.

The more US interventions caused deaths, incited and

multiplied our enemies, imposed extreme costs, and jeopardized our security, the greater my conviction became that all foreign intervention not related to our direct security should cease as quickly as possible.

The neoconservatives want an open license to go anywhere, anytime to force our "goodness" on others, even though such actions are resented and the "beneficiaries" want no part of it.

Though the foreign policy "realists" are more discretionary with their desire to intervene around the world, they nonetheless support the principle that we have the authority and obligation to be militarily engaged throughout the world. Just opening this door, even partly, supports 100 percent the principle of intervening. From there it is only a matter of degree as to when and where and how often we impose ourselves in the internal affairs of other countries and in disputes that are no concern of ours.

Once this concession is made, interventions will not remain limited, especially considering the presence of various prowar special interest groups constantly making plans to micromanage world affairs for financial reasons, as well as those driven by an addiction to using power over others.

Warfare is not unlike welfare. Once the principle of transferring wealth through government force is viewed as acceptable, it's inevitable that wealth transfers will increase until they are no longer affordable. Ironically it's the rich who end up on the receiving end more than the poor in a system supposedly designed to help the poor.

My exposure to Washington politics never tempted me to consider supporting a foreign policy of military and economic intervention. My foreign policy views in 1973, the first year I campaigned for Congress, were not as firmly developed as when I left Congress in January of 2013; experience and exposure to pro-peace journalists and authors helped strengthen my opposition to the status quo foreign policy of the Democrats and Republicans.

A time to gain, a time to lose
A time to rend, a time to sew
A time for love, a time for hate
A time for peace, I swear it's not too late!

"Turn! Turn! Turn!" The Byrds

4

Peace Is the Answer

The moral, constitutional, economic, and practical arguments against the ease with which we have gone to war are powerful and compelling. It continually baffles me that so many members of Congress are so easily influenced by the special-interest lobbyists and war propagandists and succumb to the lies told to gain support for senseless waste of lives and wealth in wars. Deceiving Americans into believing the wars are necessary to protect our freedom and the Constitution is a mockery of the truth. The propagandists seek to fool the people into believing it is patriotic to support the wars. But, the opposite is the truth: it is patriotic to support peace.

The economic cost for all war expenditures are almost totally ignored by professed conservative leaders who constantly preach fiscal restraint. This inconsistent attitude has been a significant factor in moving the US toward the national bankruptcy we now face. Cataclysmic economic decline as a consequence of excessive spending and decreased production cannot be prevented without addressing the problems brought on by our foreign policy of intervention.

Though the people are naturally opposed to offensive wars, their support eventually comes as a consequence of the persistent, daily barrage of lies about dangers we face and calls for patriotic loyalty to the warmongering leadership. The solution is for more people to seek the plain truth. It will remain difficult for this to happen if we continue to prosecute the whistle-blowers who reveal the truth of the tragic consequences related to our foreign entanglements and aggression.

The common people of all nations have always preferred peace, harmony, and prosperity over war. War propaganda, however, can overwhelm the natural inclination to seek peace. The use and exaggeration of fear stirs the emotions and hatred of those who ultimately end up suffering, dying, and paying for the wars that should have been avoided. The worst part is that the initiators of the war plans profit while the innocent suffer and die.

Much effort over the centuries has been expended to get the people to accept the notion that war is inevitable and peace is impossible.

It has often been acknowledged that the Bible says there will always be "wars and rumors of wars." Some have estimated that over the last 5,000 years over 14,000 wars have been fought, causing more than three and a half billion deaths. In our own history between 1798 and 2015, the US has used military force abroad 369 times in wars and other "situations of military conflict or potential conflict or for other than normal peacetime purposes" according to a Congressional Research Service report. That's more than one and a half instances per year. So far the certainty of war is readily apparent. But must it continue to be so? Is it possible for the basic nature of man to change? I think it can.

Think of how man's knowledge and scientific achievement have evolved—especially in just the last few hundred years—and how much the world has changed after thousands of years of relative stagnation. Why should we accept the premise that social and interpersonal relationships cannot improve in the same miraculous manner?

Though I'm sure wars and rumors of wars will continue, this need not thwart an optimistic effort to reduce the carnage of war and ensure that a lot less wars occur.

At the present time history is on the side of perpetual war. But history was on the side of man never flying in airplanes up to just a little over 100 years ago, and certainly there were no expectations at that time that we would be landing on the moon a mere 66 years after the Wright brothers' first flight.

Isaiah and the Prince of Peace

Isaiah was more optimistic about war and peace—though prematurely. Isaiah 2:4 says, "The Lord will mediate between nations and will settle international disputes. They will hammer their swords into plowshares and their spears into pruning hooks. Nation will no longer fight against nation, nor train for war anymore."

Mocking modern day religionists who champion war, the band Brave Saint Saturn satirically alters these words in the song "Blessed Are the Land Mines":To hate war is to hate usIf you love peace, then you must love treasonBeat your plowshares into swordsBeat your pulpits, turn your tablesBlessed are the hand grenadesBless the church who rattles sabers

Did not Jesus admonish and restrain Peter when, in the defense of Jesus, Peter used a sword in an effort to prevent Jesus's arrest? Jesus quickly rebuked him, saying, "Those who use the sword will die by the sword."

Though the Old Testament is filled with violence, there is no evidence Christianity in any way promotes war and violence as a solution to any of our problems. There is also no biblical instruction that we should ignore the goal of peace. Christ never taught us to hate or kill our enemies. Rather he taught us to love them. We should not assume that it is impossible to achieve this. Jesus was the Prince of Peace, not the champion of war.

Flying in airplanes along with space exploration are recent man-generated scientific marvels. Why give up on seeking a more peaceful and prosperous world? Who knows with certainty that it cannot be achieved with an advancement of human understanding and a change in the perception of what the proper role of government ought to be?

One great obstacle to peace is that both sides of most wars claim God is on their side. Even the Nazis claimed God was on their side, and were supported by some Christian ministers. The US has not been immune from making these claims, even when we go 6,000 miles from our shores to initiate wars against people who have never threatened us. The Christian church has not done well in arguing the case for peace. From the ancient crusades to the current ones going on in the Middle East, the wars have encountered too little resistance from the church. Today some evangelical Christians are among the most vocal supporters of the neoconservatives-driven wars in the Middle East.

The Christian spirit tried to break through on that one special Christmas Eve in 1914 when the Christian soldiers refused to fight and against orders called a halt to the killing as the soldiers faced off with each other on the western front. They joined each other, sang Christmas carols, and exchanged gifts of food and souvenirs. This was a moment of peace in the midst of a horrible, insane, useless war. The propagandists insisted on war; the soldiers rebelled—at least on this one occasion.

This spontaneous expression and desire for peace must be encouraged by all those who have come to know the destructive evil of war, especially those who claim a Christian faith.

The government leaders want no part of peace when they have a war to be fought. It is probably more accurate to assume that God and the Prince of Peace are on neither side. War is unholy and makes no sense. Though much killing is justified by the believers in almost all religions, it is not a theological principle of any of the world's great religions that God instructs people to seek out and start wars in order to improve the world.

It's rather amazing that there is such a disconnect between professed beliefs and the violence that occurs when both sides in a war are convinced they are on God's side.

Swiss neutrality

If there have actually been more than 14,000 wars in the past 5,000 years, little time is left for any significant periods of peace. But some countries have enjoyed peace more than the rest.

In modern times Switzerland has a reputation for having the good sense to stay out of the senseless killing. This is a remarkable feat considering that the two major world wars in the 20th century engulfed Europe.

Some argue the neutrality is only a result of geography. The surrounding mountains, it is claimed, protect Switzerland against armies invading. But there has to be more to it than that. In the age of airplanes, ICBMs, and drones, no one is safe from a determined enemy's attack.

Besides, the US has had a tremendous advantage with the

vast protection from great bodies of water to the east and west and no threats coming from our neighbors either north or south. Yet we have fought wars almost constantly—all in the name of righteousness.

Switzerland in the center of Europe survived unscathed during the 20th century carnage of two world wars—choosing a policy of neutrality. The US, in contrast, has constantly ignored the strong advice of our early leaders, and frequently the voice of the people, to stay out of the internal affairs of other nations and avoid entangling alliances. This combined with a supposed God-directed "Manifest Destiny," a neoconservative obsession with provoking wars, and an excessive spirit of nationalism and jingoism has led to our many wars throughout the world over the past 100 years.

The Swiss have not expressed this same attitude. Basically they stay at home while we march around the world looking for "monsters to destroy."

The argument goes that Switzerland is a small country and does not have the same moral responsibility that the US has as a superpower. But size is irrelevant. Great Britain is a small country that once ruled across the world with a giant empire. There's no logical argument that says the US cannot and should not have a foreign policy closer to the Swiss model than the model of the Roman Empire or even the Soviet Union.

Come you masters of war
You that build all the guns
You that build the death planes
You that build all the bombs
You that hide behind walls
You that hide behind desks
I just want you to know
I can see through your masks.

"Masters of War" Bob Dylan

5

Why Do the People Support the Wars?

A large majority of the people who fight and die in, and pay for, a war also condone the war. Otherwise the wars would cease. It's been that way for thousands of years as described in the song "Universal Soldier" by Buffy Sainte-Marie. Her claim is that without the "universal soldier" there would be no war.

But without him how would Hitler
Have condemned him at Dachau?
Without him Caesar would have stood alone

He's the one who gives his body
As a weapon to the war,
And without him all this killing can't go on

Her claim is that all of us are the universal soldiers as we ignore, condone, encourage, and justify wars that have persisted for so long. Though governments start the wars, there would be many less wars if the people would demand that the wars be rare and justified and if the people refused to be deceived by the war propaganda and the special interests that maneuver us into war.

Man's social relationships have made no progress if the number of human beings killed by other human beings is any measurement. The fact that wars in the 20th century generated the slaughter of tens of millions of people is beyond comprehension and ignored by supporters of new wars. It will be even harder to get people to oppose war now that wars are fought with modern technology, including drones. War will never be rejected unless we adopt a completely new approach that strictly limits government war-making powers and the people exercise the courage to refuse to support the government whenever those powers are exceeded.

Why do people succumb to the commands of the promoters of illegitimate war? If governments were denied the cannon fodder and the wealth required to pursue wars, a lot fewer wars would be fought. Most wars are justified through deceptions, and the deceptions feed on themselves. Where there is true one-sided blame, it would be a justifiable defensive war for the country attacked.

Some argue that there is always one side to blame for the aggression. Others deny that their own nation's failed policies and aggressive behaviors create any responsibility for war. Emotions and sudden events prevent people from developing a reasoned understanding of the circumstances leading up to a conflict. For instance, World War II cannot be understood without understanding World War I. Also, refusing to deal with the blowback phenomenon makes it impossible to sort out truth from fiction on just who's responsible for the breakout of hostilities.

There is rarely just one reason given to encourage the people to support war. Inevitably, creating war support among the people requires official lies to build the fear needed to get the average person to reject peace as preferable to war. In a defensive war the invasion is obvious and official lies are not required.

The hardest lie to overcome is the lie the promoters accept themselves. Though ulterior motives exist, war promoters tend to find it easier to adapt their thoughts in line with the lies they use to justify war than to admit, if only to themselves, the truth. Even the worst dictators convince themselves that their war mission is justified, if not noble. Does anyone think the war promoters in or out of government, such as the neoconservatives who provoked the Iraq and Afghanistan wars, have a sense of guilt for the carnage and the economic havoc their wars have brought?

Though a war may have been initiated for reasons related to oil, the military-industrial complex, Israel, vengeance, or ignorance regarding blowback, it is still required that the people be convinced there's a noble, though false, purpose behind the war. Propaganda must also give the people a reason—entirely made up if necessary—to fear an enemy presented as about to attack us. It always works that way.

War propaganda is always used to gain public support by overcoming the natural tendency of most people to prefer peace and prosperity over war and death.

If the process for gaining support of the people for unnecessary wars is not understood, it will be virtually impossible to expect civilization to move in the direction of fewer wars. Only by revealing the real reasons for initiating war can we refute the war propagandists and reduce the frequency of war.

The actual motives for war are many and varied. Pure aggression to expand borders without extenuating circumstances is rare. Even Hitler and Stalin claimed, and maybe even believed, they were acting in the defense of their countries and that war was needed to rectify previous grievances and provide protection for their citizens.

Today the three countries that we are being conditioned to fear the most as potential military attackers are Iran, Russia, and China. The process of disinformation continues to prepare the American people for war against these nations just as it did for war against Iraq, Afghanistan, Libya, and Syria.

Ironically, while we're constantly being warned about the military threats of others who are about to attack us, our political leaders continue to engage in constant wars to expand our empire for various reasons throughout the world. The war propagandists—whether from politics, industry, academia, or media—conspire to convince the people, who initially resist wars, to support the war effort because it will protect us from possible attack. The early resistance is overcome. Resistance often reemerges later when the economic suffering and the number of people killed and wounded are realized—always too late.

Why do the people succumb to war propaganda? The reason is not that people trust in government. The majority of Americans believe our leaders constantly lie to them. Congress's approval rating is 15% or less. Yet the people hardly ever resist the call to arms. Irrespective of initial resistance, they are willing to send young men and women halfway around the world to fight and die in undeclared, illogical, unconstitutional wars against non-enemies who have never attacked us. Why?

Unlike any prior US war, today we have a global war with a fuzzy beginning and no strategy for an ending against an un-identifiable enemy. It looks like Orwell in his novel 1984 was right about perpetual war for perpetual peace. On purpose, the elusive peace is never realized.

Certain conditions must exist for the people to be persuaded to support a war that challenges their natural instincts. It all starts with the motivation of elites in power who do not highly value liberty for the average person. Instead, these elites primarily desire securing their power or wealth. This is the one area where governments are efficient, and the people negligent.

The war propagandists must instill fear and get the people to demand that the government make them safe. When these conditions are achieved the people eagerly give up their liberty as a "patriotic duty."

For the authoritarians to convince the people that war is necessary to provide safety, the authoritarians present a common enemy whose defeat requires the people to sacrifice respect for their natural right to their lives and liberty.

The authoritarians are mainly concerned with their power. They know well what Randolph Bourne revealed in his essay "The State": "War is the health of the State." Controlling the people—the sacrificial lambs—is done in part by repeating that patriotism requires that we all unite behind the government to defeat a common foreign enemy.

Because their goals driving policy are counter to the people's interests, it should not be a surprise that governments lie to the people to obtain support for perpetual war. Journalist I. F. Stone warned: "Every government is run by liars and nothing they say should be believed."

The neoconservatives' love of war

The neoconservatives are among the principal proponents of our current foreign policy and the constant wars it generates. President George W. Bush on June 18, 2002 fulfilled Orwell's warning of government proclaiming that war is peace when Bush stated, "I just want you to know that, when we talk about war, we're really talking about peace." And I'm sure Bush believed this and lost no sleep over the carnage and destruction he generated in Iraq and Afghanistan.

Archneoconservative and great admirer of Machiavelli, Michael Ledeen, vehemently defends this grotesque philosophy. In his book *Machiavelli on Modern Leadership*, Ledeen writes, "Thus, paradoxically, peace increases our peril, by making discipline less urgent, encouraging some of our worst instincts, and depriving us of some of our best leaders." He praises Prussian General Helmuth von Moltke for stating that "Everlasting peace is a dream, not even a pleasant one; war is a necessary part of God's arrangements of the world.... Without war the world would deteriorate into materialism." Ledeen says that material abundance should not be preferred to the death and destruction of war. This makes no sense.

Ledeen says Machiavelli argued that "peace undermines discipline and thereby gives the destructive vices greater sway." Machiavelli, in Ledeen's interpretation, is incensed that peace is the enemy of the all-important state and represents a great danger. Ledeen basically praises war for what Randolph Bourne wisely noted is one of war's greatest detriments—that war nourishes the state.

It boils down to the fact that some people, including the neocons, hold God-like beliefs about the state while others concern themselves with the God-given rights of all people to life and liberty.

The statists often win with their aggressive approach to defending their authority and the rest of the people pay, not willing to withhold their support from the state. How could the warmongers fight wars if money and troops were withheld from the "Prince?"

The hypocrisy of the instigators of wars should be enough to awaken the people to reject the war profiteers. The true warmongers rarely die in war, nor even serve in the military. But, they reap the material benefits of the wars they provoke and promote.

The chickenhawks of today should be held in contempt. Those who promote war, but never participate in war, should be seen for what they are—hypocrites of the worst kind. This is especially true for all the neocon warmongers who managed to get deferments from the draft.

In contrast, individuals like Muhammad Ali consistently refused to be drafted to fight and said no one else should be forced to fight either.

Multiple times Dick Cheney and other current war promoters sought refuge from the dangers of a war similar to the wars they eagerly supported later on. Refusing to participate in an unjust, undeclared war like Vietnam is not being "chicken." To do that takes courage, something the chickenhawks are devoid of. Prison and even death can result from refusing to fight in an unjust war. Chickenhawks, in contrast, rarely suffer any consequence.

Check the military service of other war promoters including Bill Bennett, Paul Wolfowitz, Richard Perle, Elliott Abrams, Bill Kristol, Robert Kagan, David Wurmser, Scooter Libby, Norman Podhoretz, John Podhoretz, James Schlesinger, Dov Zakheim, Douglas Feith, Michael Ledeen, and David Frum.

Proponents of war and violence can sometimes be very revealing when they blurt out the truth. Hermann Goering, in his classic quote on war propaganda, was unseemly blunt and honest. Osama bin Laden, to my knowledge, never lied about his reasons for supporting the 9/11 attack. But our leaders were deaf to bin Laden's revelations.

What is scary is how Goering concludes that "it is always a simple matter to drag the people along, whether it is a democracy or a fascist dictatorship or a Parliament or a Communist dictatorship." His advice: Lie to them; tell the people "they are being attacked and denounce the pacifists for lack of patriotism and exposing the country to danger. It works the same way in any country." Considering Goering's war propaganda explanation, I am reminded of all of the denunciations of those who opposed the fighting and killing of the last couple of decades, especially in the run-up to wars in Iraq and Afghanistan.

Spreading truth can build resistance to war

Human nature never seems to change. But must it always be that way? All we need are more people, and maybe a generation of young people, who are willing to demand reason over war propaganda's plays on emotions, willing to reject the lies in which the beneficiaries of war engage. If the truth is known, resistance will build. Resistance builds, for example, when the people tire of a longtime dictator or any authoritarian system. Eventually the people's voices are heard. This fact, in itself, has overthrown dictators. But why not sooner rather than later? Does the delay come from weak reasoning, lack of proper leadership, apathy, or just plain gullibility?

Yes, we know that the war propagandists have the edge, with help from the government bully pulpit, the media, and, to a degree, Hollywood. But, today WE have the internet with which to compete. Also we have a disgusted populous and a generation of young people sick and tired of the lies, poverty, and war that government policies have generated. If we have a generation of young people who can revolutionize their attitudes about perpetual government propaganda, war, and insidious poverty, things will change for the better.

Getting people to support a war, especially those who have to fight and sacrifice so much, requires generating fear of and hatred against an enemy—an enemy about which the people often know very little. Many lies have to be told to frighten the people to support wars. Recall the lies and hysteria surrounding the buildup for both the Persian Gulf War and, twelve years later, the Iraq War. It was incessant, and the prowar politicians, as well as former military members who had moved on to jobs with war industry companies, were accommodated by a compliant media. To keep the propaganda alive after hostilities erupted, the journalists "embedded" themselves in the military and reported only what was approved by our military and political leaders.

History shows that demonizing an enemy through lies and gross distortions can gain popular support for war. This phenomenon was required even in our Civil War. How else would it have been possible for a country to succumb to so much self-mutilation with over 700,000 fighters dying and hundreds of thousands wounded?

We're living in a period where demonization of Muslims and Arabs is epidemic and growing. How else can support for the never-ending Global War on Terror be maintained? Fear, hatred, and vengeance are required to keep the killing going. It is not only the enemy that is killed as a consequence; many Americans suffer and die as well.

We believe everything they tell us
They're gonna' kill us
So we gotta' kill them first
But I remember a commandment
Thou shalt not kill
How much is that soldier's life worth?
And what ever happened to peace on earth?

"What Ever Happened to Peace on Earth?" Willie Nelson

6

Pursuing US Empire

The incitement to perpetual war has been achieved without an actual threat to our security. We have not engaged in hostilities with any nation since 1945 that was capable of doing harm to us, and yet there has been plenty of fighting and killing in the last 70 years. The only nation that was capable in this period of harming us was the Soviet Union, and we steered clear of fighting the Soviet Union.

Our obsession with expanding our sphere of influence around the world was designed to promote an empire. It was never for true national security purposes.

To keep hatred and thus war alive, the propagandists must stay active.

I'd like to believe that reason would be enough to change the people's attitudes about war, yet an attitude change is more likely to occur in conjunction with a bankruptcy that forces us to come to our senses and abandon our obsession for an ever-expanding world empire.

Tyrants and aggressors usually cling to "philosophers" or "learned scholars" to defend their use of war as a political tool. Sometimes the philosophers are explicit in endorsing the use of force. Other times what those philosophers say and believe will be adapted so the tyrant can be "defended" by an intellectual.

Throughout history references have been made to Nietzsche, Rousseau, Hegel, Marx, and other philosophers to justify war. Some neoconservatives even use Christianity to justify wars—making a call for a type of modern Christian crusade.

The dictators who instigate wars never preach nonviolence and peaceful resistance as did Gandhi and Martin Luther King, Jr. The efforts of Gandhi and King, though, show what can be achieved without an army and by people armed with only confidence in their view that setting an example and exercising persuasion can change the world.

The French Jacobins' philosophy behind US Empire

The US government's philosophic support for recent aggressive moves around the world can be traced back to the Jacobins of the French Revolution. Though Rousseau is linked to the crimes of that revolution, he himself would not likely have interpreted his ideas as did Robespierre in the Reign of Terror. Robespierre expressed in 1794 his view that "terror is only justice prompt, severe and inflexible; it is then an emanation of virtue…" War, one must know, is peace! The Jacobins' strong belief that using such prompt and severe force to "do good" is the exact opposite of the philosophy of nonviolence and peaceful resistance that Gandhi and King advocated.

Today, according to Claes Ryn in his 2011 book *The New Jacobinism: America as Revolutionary State*, the neoconservatives have adopted a philosophy quite similar to that of the French Jacobins.

The neocons' current "guillotine" is the drone missile, which serves as a powerful substitute to make their point. The policy of kill lists and assassinations, unless it's strongly refuted, could morph into a much more widely applied system of "justice prompt, severe and inflexible."

Executions in the Reign of Terror required no trial, nor did they adhere to any rule of law. Today the kill lists are drafted and the executions in foreign lands are carried out in secret. Ryn has it right: it's clear that the neoconservatives have a philosophic outlook similar to the Jacobins.

Irving Kristol was recognized as the "godfather of the most powerful new political force in America—neo-conservativism" in Esquire magazine in 1979. Kristol, a follower of Leo Strauss, was instrumental in that revolution of the latter part of the 20th century. I see our job as making certain that the neoconservatives' revolutionary movement ends in its deserved failure.

Neoconservatives, like Jacobins, endorse the principle of using whatever force is needed to impose their will. Neoconservatives are dedicated to using force to spread American "exceptionalism and goodness" around the world. This has caused a great deal of suffering for the world and America. Although neoconservatives are recent advocates, their program is quite similar to Woodrow Wilson's desire, expressed in his April 2, 1917 war advocacy speech to a joint session of Congress, that "[t]he world must be made safe for democracy." Always the self-proclaimed "humanitarians" are the ones who have a guillotine or other weapon to back up their vision for the world. This method eventually ends badly; Robespierre lost his head over it literally.

Only via a better idea, presented persuasively, can we expect long-lasting changes to come about with little violence.

The Jacobins of 18th century France did not last long. Let's make certain that the new Jacobins' days of influence end soon. It's time to bury all the "guillotines" and promote the cause of liberty through nonviolent persuasion.

International arrangements advancing war

It's not that there have not been efforts made to promote peace; it's just that there's been so little success. A few countries have taken a different approach and avoided to some degree active participation in war. Sweden and Switzerland have maintained neutrality rather than joining the bloody slugfests in the 20th century. But many nations were involved in the extreme violence and killing associated with war in the 20th century. Many efforts by the non-aligned countries to remain neutral during the Cold War were also subverted by the aggressive nature of the foreign policies of both the Soviets and the United States.

Peace treaties at the conclusion of wars are supposed to restore peace. Yet they are too often just about redrawing national boundaries and rewarding the victors. This leads to problems later. The declared successes associated with the Treaty of Versailles after World War I turned out to be nothing more than a lull in the fighting. The treaty's harsh treatment of the war's losers to benefit the winners helped create instabilities that guaranteed World War II.

After World War I, an attempt to resolve conflicts without war with the League of Nations failed outright. Then, after World War II the United Nations was established with a stated goal of being a peacekeeping council. Less than five years after the UN was established, it sanctioned the Korean War via a series of Security Council resolutions in June and July of 1950. The US illegally joined the war without a congressional declaration of war. The purported peace-promoting organization gave Truman cover to jump into what was really a civil war over efforts to reunite the Korean people in one nation. The splitting up of Korea after World War II, half for the Soviets and half for the US allies, was the cause of the war. Peace efforts after World War II were mediocre and only set the stage for war.

It's safe to say that peace treaties and international organizations purportedly designed for peace, like United Nations, are more likely to serve powerful special interests than prevent war. They too often end up buttressing war.

Multilateral treaties to "stop aggression" actually often are not designed for peace. They are designed instead to intimidate and threaten a nation or nations into agreeing to the demands of those who reap rewards from war profiteering, including through gaining land and obtaining access to natural resources.

Senator Robert Taft argued against NATO out of concern that it would be a tool for war rather than for peace. Not only is our sovereignty sacrificed and the Congress ignored under such international treaties, the alliances built through them pull us into more war—not less.

Recent history shows NATO—which is US-directed since the US provides a disproportionate share of the money and troops—has gone to war in Bosnia-Herzegovina, Afghanistan, and Libya. Plus, NATO keeps the agitation going against Russia with a demand that missiles be placed in Eastern Europe. And soon it could be NATO "peace" efforts that will get us deeper into wars in Syria and Ukraine.

While the risk of military conflict with Russia related to Ukraine is easy to see, the US involvement in Syria could also be the one that will not be contained. Not only might the military action linger as it did in Afghanistan, it may spread and bring the Russians in in opposition, creating a much bigger war than anyone so far has imagined. Unfortunately, the temporary reprieve from the US bombing Syria lasted less than a year.

The tendency of multinational agreements and organizations to advance war, even if their stated purposes involve promoting peace, arises from the nature of government. By their very nature governments are opposed to peaceful resolution. Their goal is strictly to solidify power and gain economic advantage. Governments have always been in the business of war. They will not deliver peace. Most people naively believe that governments intend to promote peace, liberty, and security. It's more accurate to say governments use force, including war, to secure power and wealth for a privileged class at the expense of the rest of the people.

There will always be a claimed danger lurking out there of a "Hitler" who has to be stopped. Safety from the bad guys will motivate the people to support propagandists' calls for war.

Even when there is a lull in the killing, the weapons of war are still manufactured. But weapons limitation agreements do not work. For one thing, weapons don't cause war; governments managed by people who devise bad policies do. Military might and disarmament treaties are not as crucial as is the sincerity of the people and the government in their rejection of aggression.

Hope and confidence must be realistic. There can be no self-deception as to the expectations related to governments run by individuals whose goal in life is to seek power and wealth. For peace to ever break out, the prevailing sentiment has to be the rejection of the initiation of force against others.

War, huh, good God y'all
What is it good for?
Absolutely nothing, say it again
War, whoa, Lord
What is it good for?
Absolutely nothing, listen to me

"War" Edwin Starr

7

The War Issue

The issue of war has been discussed since the beginning of recorded history 5,000 years ago. Though bits and pieces of people's existence prior to written history are known, there is not clear evidence of organized warfare prior to 5,000 years ago. Surviving nature's challenges, not organized warfare, probably preoccupied prehistoric people. Some claim the existence of weapons and battles over hunting grounds and food at a tribal level most likely existed. No doubt man's violence against one another has been around from the beginning of man's existence on earth.

Recorded history of the past 5,000 years shows ample evidence that military conquests were used to expand small cities into larger cities and, as early as the third millennium BC, even into empires. It seems that the history of the human race is intertwined with the history of war. But must it remain that way forever?

People have evolved from the early stages of a primitive bare existence to the amazing advanced industrial society that we have today. In the last few hundred years alone we have witnessed an amazing technological advancement. Many of the major technological changes have occurred in the last 260 years and have been associated with the Industrial Revolution. Mankind has made great strides in the areas of technology, scientific breakthroughs, and material abundance in an amazingly short period of time.

There are many who have made a point that the Christian emphasis on the responsibility and importance of each individual, the principle of free will, or a work ethic associated with the Protestant Reformation significantly contributed to the Industrial Revolution and the technological progress of the recent past. If Christian thought contributed to economic prosperity, it did it through an emphasis on individual freedom and a free-market economy. It is the relationship of people's technological progress and the general advancement of the material well-being of the developed nations of the world to the issue of war that raises many questions.

War is economically destructive

It has been argued that war is a major reason, if not the most significant reason, especially in the past 100 years, that the material advance has been so great. But could it be that it is in spite of the coercive investment of the state in war that the benefits to society have continued? The material benefits may well have been even greater without the death and destruction of the past 100 years of wars that should not have been waged.

Would not the jet engine still have been developed without a need for a faster fighter plane? Without NASA, would not the "spinoffs" have been just as significant with space exploration left to private resources?

As Randolph Bourne wrote, war is the "health of the state." Tyranny results from war. War is always an economic negative. Even a purely defensive war destroys wealth.

Liberty, markets, property, honest money, and peace generate prosperity. In contrast, war distracts from wealth creation, consumes wealth, and undermines liberty. I see no evidence that war in any way contributes to prosperity. Absent war, prosperity would occur anyway and to an even greater extent. With war there is always less wealth overall, though the war profiteers always benefit.

War in the age of plenty

For hundreds of years there have been tremendous material improvements for mankind. Civilization has advanced, yet, at the same time, wars have become more destructive than ever. This lack of progress in dealing with government-sponsored wars has allowed the killing and maiming of hundreds of millions of people in the past 100 years. Technological progress went into more sophisticated methods for killing one another, through means including nuclear and chemical warfare, genocide, deliberate starvation, and now "sterile," sophisticated drone warfare.

Technologically the human race has achieved amazing success. Yet all too often this success has been canceled out by war and destruction. Can we advance technology and peace together, showering millions of average people with grandiose benefits of which even kings of old could never have dreamed?

We can exalt progress in science, knowledge, and material benefits. But we should also be concerned regarding the static state or even decline of the human character. It seems the richer the world is with material possessions and opportunities, the more violent society becomes as people make no progress in seeking peace. The poor in America have cell phones, TVs, and cars, yet US wars remain commonplace.

There should be less reason now than in any time in our history for people to seek abundance through plunder. There is no need to steal food with the knowledge we have today regarding how to produce. The benefits of free trade and the principle of property rights proved that Thomas Malthus and Paul Ehrlich were wrong. Yet many are still starving around the world, victims of war and governments restraining free markets and property rights.

Wealth in America is largely due to a heritage of significant government respect for individual rights. The more authoritarian and socialized a society becomes, the greater is the number of poor people. Certainly the prosperity America has benefited from in the last couple hundred years did not include the socialized Indian reservations.

If we think it routine to remotely make a spacecraft land on and drive around Mars, as well as to walk on the moon, how can there be a need to plunder for food and natural resources? Once it's understood how production and distribution can be achieved in peace, hunger and poverty can be dealt with much more efficiently.

Science and knowledge have offered so much to us already in material abundance. Why is it that we cannot consider the advancement of the human character to a different stage where the notion that war is necessary is overcome?

There is obviously a serious disconnect between people's development in scientific understanding, which has raised the standard of living for many, and people's moral maturity in understanding and doing something about those who promote war, torture, aggression, assassinations, and war profiteering.

The free market allows for mass production and techno-logical advancements, which we have clearly witnessed. But without an improvement in man's moral behavior, we end up using modern technology for making mass killings more effi-cient and supporting the war profiteers who constantly agitate for wars and generate threats of wars. Wouldn't it be better to use this technology to spread prosperity instead of destruction?

The choice need not be limited to scientific advancement with war. It must be asked how we can seek advancement in the cause of peace without giving up scientific progress. Not only would we not need to give up the scientific progress and ad-vancement of material abundance of the world, we would see a greater material abundance if the human race could adapt to a moral system. Nuclear power can be used for making bombs, or it can be used for the generation of electricity, which has been done quite frequently in the last 60 years. Wisdom, char-acter, and morality are needed in the intellectual leadership to work for a society where the energy wasted to pursue war is instead used to pursue prosperity.

In all of recorded history it seems that people's moral char-acter has not evolved in a positive way. Even with the great religions teaching love, compassion, and respect for others, consistent with the Golden Rule, there has essentially been no progress. The killing only becomes more sophisticated and in-tense with scientific advancements.

We cannot continue to focus on using the great scientific achievements to kill more efficiently. This moral flaw must be overcome, or the human race will destroy itself. It's time to slow down the development of weapons of war and see if man is capable of moving in the direction of peace. The message of liberty and peace must be spread throughout the world in order to achieve greater prosperity worldwide and benefit the hungry and the poor.

Killing in the name of God

The great religions present a case for love, justice, and peace. But, other than in a few cases, the religious beliefs, no matter how well intended, have contributed little to peace and prosperity.

Religion has been hijacked by the nonbelievers and used to support war. It has been claimed in most wars that God is on both sides. In theory the Jewish, Christian, and Muslim God is the same; yet think of all the killing that has gone on in the name of God. To some this is an argument against the whole notion of spiritual beliefs, but that ignores the differences between the original religious beliefs and how they have been twisted to become tools of those motivated by power, hate, and violence.

Power-seekers concentrate on materialism and accept the principle of government redistribution as legitimate. For them the redistribution becomes a moral good. However, in a society that rejects violence as a proper tool for improving well-being, such redistribution is called theft. Indeed the rich and politically connected soon use redistribution to benefit themselves, leaving the poor worse off than they would otherwise have been.

Even those avowed atheists prone to war create their own "God" as did the communists who ruled the Soviet Union for a large part of the 20th century. It continues to exist in many countries today where the state itself becomes the "God" that then undermines the peace message of the major religions.

The neocons in the run-up to the Iraq War manipulated religion to justify war. Archneoconservative Michael Ledeen in his book on Machiavelli made it clear that religious beliefs and religious fervor were to be used to support the state and the wars it perpetrates instead of as instruments of love and compassion in the cause of peace—professed goals of Christianity.

These manipulations are not evidence that evil is a result of religious beliefs. Instead, they show how evil men usurp the authority of religion to promote war. That this tactic can succeed reflects that too much complacency among people is preventing resistance against the thugs who coopt religion and use it for evil ends.

A revolutionary change in attitude

The question remains: Why has there been no advancement in human relations that would promote peace while at the same time the magnificent scientific advancements continue to be used to make war more deadly, government more powerful, and the people's liberty more threatened?

Is this inevitable and merely a reflection of the true nature of man? Does this mean that the human race cannot be changed for the better by advancing knowledge and ethics to improve personal relationships and challenge the government's authority to use force without restraint? Must there always be "wars and rumors of war"? Accepting the inevitability of war is one thing, but glorifying war in the name of God and claiming that it reflects strong character and patriotism is quite another. Patriotism may well need a new definition. Samuel Johnson probably had it right calling patriotism "the last refuge of a scoundrel."

It should not be such a stretch to envision the possibility of mankind advancing to a more civilized state where human conflict is reduced. Yet, instead, man's inhumanity to man has become worse in its cruelty—especially when measured in the number of lives lost as a consequence of war in the past century. This has happened in spite of the astounding brilliance that gives us our scientific advancement.

Could it be that the most important change has to be a revolutionary change in attitude about the role of the state and its power to take the people to war? The responsibility of each individual to exert himself to remove or restrain this power is crucial.

Where have all the soldiers gone, long time passing?
Where have all the soldiers gone, long time ago?
Where have all the soldiers gone?
Gone to graveyards, everyone
Oh, when will they ever learn?
Oh, when will they ever learn?

"Where Have All the Flowers Gone?" Peter, Paul and Mary

8

Foreign Policy and War

A flawed foreign policy plants the seeds of ill-conceived wars.

The Founding Fathers had precise thoughts on the type of foreign policy to which the US should adhere. In his first inaugural address, President Thomas Jefferson concisely described the proper foreign policy as "peace, commerce, and honest friendship with all nations, entangling alliances with none." This is a great goal. But unfortunately we have not had much peace.

As great a president as Jefferson was, his speeches and writings were superior to his foreign policy as president. He was the first US president to deploy troops to fight on foreign soil. Sending marines into what is now Libya and blockading Tripoli hardly qualified as action necessary to protect US national security.

What is the fascination with Libya? Reagan on April 15, 1986 ordered a bombing raid on Tripoli and other Libya locations in which over 100 people were killed, although Libya had not attacked America. And more recently we have President Obama who ordered the bombing of Libya. In this recent offensive against Libya, Muammar Gaddafi—a target of Reagan's bombings almost thirty years earlier—was killed.

In 1807, in seeking the best policy to deal with trade with Great Britain and France who were at war with each other, Jefferson signed the Embargo Act that astoundingly prohibited trade through American ports not just with Great Britain and France but with all countries of the world. It didn't work as it was hoped it would, and Jefferson, before he left office, conceded its failure and repealed the act.

Not much has changed. A politician's performance rarely matches his promising rhetoric once he is in a position to practice what he preaches.

From peacemaker promises to war-maker reality

George W. Bush is the epitome of a candidate who does not follow his own pronouncements with regard to foreign policy once he becomes president. In the first Bush-Gore debate on October 3, 2000, Bush was eloquent, but grossly misleading, when he said, "…if we don't stop extending our troops all around the world in nation building missions, then we're going to have a serious problem coming down the road, and I'm going to prevent that." Bush also declared during the debate: "I don't want to be the world's policeman. I want to be the world's peacemaker…."

Bush was coached well, and he remembered his lines perfectly. Many people preparing to vote in the presidential election were elated to hear a message of peace. What if Bush had expressed the views of all his neoconservative advisers and told the American people the truth about the plan laid out in the Project for the New American Century, years before 9/11, to go to war to remake the entire Middle East?

In the second debate with Al Gore, Bush promoted the need for a "humble" foreign policy.

Jefferson's infractions were miniscule compared to the radical new foreign policy devised by the Bush administration. All that was to come, once Bush was in office; it was on the planning table from the beginning. September 11, 2001 turned out to be that "Pearl Harbor event" the neoconservatives were hoping for in order to prepare the American people to support the foreign policy for which the neocons longed.

Paul O'Neill, Bush's first secretary of the treasury, revealed that at the very first National Security Council meeting the subject of attacking Iraq was on the agenda for discussion. O'Neill lasted in the administration until December of 2002 when he was fired for disagreeing with Bush on the Iraq War and for expressing the danger of the large deficits. The neoconservatives who controlled the Bush administration managed to radicalize foreign policy. That foreign policy has been altered only slightly in the Obama administration.

Of major significance was the establishment of the "Bush Doctrine," which was officially announced in September 17, 2002 as the National Security Strategy of the United States of America. The Bush Doctrine was created to justify ongoing and future interventions on the basis of America's "moral" responsibility since becoming the only superpower left standing. More succinctly, the Bush Doctrine is about pursuing a world empire.

Bush had already explained to the American people three months earlier on June 1, 2002, through a West Point commencement speech, the new, radical, and dangerous policy that would guide US foreign interventions. The Bush Doctrine was needed, Bush argued, due to unbalanced dictators around the world who could deliver weapons of mass destruction anywhere in the world. He argued that the US needs to start wars to prevent wars that might happen.

If Bush had been honest with his language, he would have admitted that henceforth he believed we had an obligation to commit aggression against others who had neither attacked us nor were capable of doing so and who did not threaten our national security.

It was always President Bush's assumption that congressional declarations of war are never necessary. The Bush Doctrine views concurrence with international organizations like the UN and NATO as giving the president the political cover and authority to start a war.

Bush even argued that this power to attack a country might be used just to prevent a country from obtaining a weapon in the future. Step aside rule of law! This is extreme abuse of power at its worst!

This Bush Doctrine stands today and is assumed by President Obama to be legitimate as he carries out a secret drone war worldwide with no congressional input or oversight.

Associated with the Bush Doctrine is preemptive war, the assassination of Americans and foreigners without due process, secret military prisons, extraordinary rendition, and torture. How anyone can argue that this makes America safer and more respected is beyond me. Common sense should tell us that such actions are a sure way to create more enemies. Resentment toward the US grows with each new attack. Resentment also grows with the sweep of the US military, and US support of dictators and insurgents, around the world.

This Bush Doctrine is based on a view that there is good and evil in the world and that the United States can do no harm since we are always on the side of righteousness while the people who oppose our bombs and occupations are always the evil ones. The Bush Doctrine defends the US killing a supposed enemy 6,000 miles away who has never attacked and cannot attack America. Those who struggle and sacrifice to expel foreign invaders from their homeland are the monsters that must be stopped according to the logic of Presidents Bush and Obama, who take their cues from the neoconservatives.

The phrase used to prompt the American people to accept this radical change—adoption of an official policy of military aggression—is the "Global War on Terror." As long as what is done is in the name of this "war," no questions will be asked.

Through much of its history, the US has flaunted moral principle through a foreign policy that tolerates secret killings, propping up dictators, and using force to secure natural resources and acquire land. US interventionist foreign policy has been around for a long time, but it had often been pursued covertly. If the policy had become known, the American people might have objected, believing the policy to be wrong. It was never before an announced policy, as it is today.

Today the Bush Doctrine is official US policy, out in the open and accepted under the law with generous use of supportive presidential orders, as well as UN and NATO resolutions. Unfortunately, today it's even accepted that the Bush Doctrine supersedes the Constitution. Congressional responsibility and congressional prerogatives are abandoned. I see the Bush Doctrine as an American-style "enabling act," giving dictatorial powers to any sitting president.

The Bush Doctrine has continued in force and expanded in application under President Obama. If the Bush Doctrine is not reversed, it will become a major contributing factor one day to a financial crisis associated with a national bankruptcy. It will then invite all the peoples of the many countries that we have offended with our aggressive interventions to pile on big time. Retaliation will be vicious. All Americans will be blamed and "punished" even though the tragic mess was orchestrated by the few who manipulated foreign policy for their own benefit. The greatest fault of the American people has been that their complacency prevented effective resistance to the government overstepping its bounds and acting in a lawless manner.

Bipartisan foreign policy and suppression of dissent

Proponents of intervention have long pushed the line that foreign policy, especially during war, is supposed to be bipartisan with no dissent permitted.

Wartime presidents have been the worst in their violations of the liberty of individuals who have been critical of the government's policies. As early as 1798, a potential war with France prompted the passage of four laws known as of the Alien and Sedition Acts. The laws were promoted by the Federalists and signed by President John Adams. Such a short time transpired from the writing of the Constitution to when the protection of liberty was ignored. Under the laws, Congressman Matthew Lyon of Vermont was imprisoned for criticizing Adams. Presidents guilty of First Amendment violations include Lincoln, Wilson, FDR, and our current President Barack Obama, as well as George W. Bush. Wartime presidents have been notorious for such abuses. Fortunately, by 1802 three of the four Alien and Sedition Acts had expired or were repealed. But, more liberty suppressing wartime legislation of later presidencies remains in force.

Today both the Democratic and Republican parties support the expansive US Empire as well as the neoconservatives' agitation for a perpetual Global War on Terror. The disagreement we hear between the two parties is only regarding management style and is designed to use political failures and un-intended consequences to enhance the power and influence of one party relative to the other.

Nothing ever seems to change in US politics—for the better at least. Today's political environment has allowed for continued abuse of presidential powers—Associated Press reporters being spied on, the Benghazi cover-up, use of the IRS to punish political enemies, surveillance of all Americans under the authority of the PATRIOT Act, and the secret FISA court rulings to mention a few.

Our government over many years has increasingly ignored the Fourth Amendment. It abuses the privacy of citizens while protecting the secrecy of its own illegal behavior. Congressional investigations and commissions mostly protect the guilty government officials. Meanwhile, whistle-blowers, who are supposedly protected by law, are punished for revealing the truth to the people.

Woodrow Wilson, shortly after maneuvering us into World War I (the greatest foreign policy mistake of the 20th century), encouraged Congress to pass and signed into law a new version of a sedition act, called the Espionage Act of 1917. The new First Amendment suppression law was used by Wilson to silence dissenters against the ill-conceived US involvement in World War I. For example, Eugene V. Debs, who had run for president four times, was prosecuted and put in a federal prison for speaking out against the war. Interestingly, it took a Republican "conservative" President Warren Harding to commute the sentence and release the socialist Debs in 1921. Unlike the Alien and Sedition Acts, the Espionage Act stayed on the books.

Don't let bad laws hang around

Obama, through Attorney General Eric Holder, rejuvenated the Espionage Act, using it more than any president since Wilson. On seven occasions the Obama administration has used the Espionage Act to charge government officials for leaks to the media. It has also used the law to justify seizing emails and phone records of Associated Press and Fox News reporters.

Bad laws should never be written, and they wouldn't be if politicians adhered to the Constitution. And if bad laws are written, the solution is to repeal them quickly and completely. Don't let the bad laws hang around. Get rid of them! Otherwise, they are bound to be used by another authoritarian president later on.

Witness what harm has come from the de facto "laws" that permit presidentially-inspired preemptive war and assassinations. The wars that are pursued without proper congressional approval should always be referred to as initiating aggression against non-threatening enemies, to make sure everybody knows exactly what we're talking about.

Preemptive or preventive war is now accepted by both political parties. It is also accepted by all branches of our government. Likewise, assassinations, secret military tribunals, and torture are now identified worldwide as policies acceptable to the US government and the American people. The image of the US throughout the world, and especially in the Middle East, is more negative now than at any time in our nation's history.

Many Americans have at the same time exhibited a general willingness to give up liberty for safety. We have ignored the warnings of the Founders that the loss of liberty leads to the loss of security as well.

The world slips from US control

Our leaders have delivered to us unlimited foreign entanglements. It is often believed that, as long as we're the economic powerhouse of the world and have a huge military advantage, we can control the world by "owning" international organizations like the United Nations, NATO, the IMF, and the World Bank. These international organizations may also be used as a means to get around congressional oversight and restrictions that Congress and the people might prefer. To a degree, that control has been achieved. But now that the US is the largest debtor nation in the world and in all history, the days of military and economic supremacy are numbered, as are the days of dollar hegemony.

Major adjustments to the balance of world power and national boundaries are inevitable. Our domination of world events cannot be maintained by increasing spending, borrowing, and money printing. The sooner we realize that the course on which we have embarked is extremely dangerous the better off we'll be. Denial is not a solution.

Governments naturally lie to maintain power. Eventually the deception perpetrated is believed by the government officials themselves. This encourages them to continue a failed policy until it's too late. Ego plays a large part in it as well.

It's highly likely that our policy of foreign intervention will not be reversed and that world chaos will result as a new world order sets in—and it won't be the New World Order that interventionists have promoted for so many years.

It was encouraging to see the results of a Pew Research Center survey released in December of 2013. For the first time in the over fifty years the survey question had been asked the majority of Americans agreed that the United States should "mind its own business" in international affairs. It was music to my ears, to say the least. This, I'm sure, represents a philosophic change with regard to our foreign policy as well as a realization that we can no longer afford all our overseas activities. US foreign policy's loss of credibility around the world contributes to this remarkable change of attitude. Hopefully, that means we're coming closer to the day our troops can "just march home."

We sell 'em missiles, we sell 'em tanks
We give 'em credit, you can call up the bank
It's just a business, you can pay us in crude
You'll love these toys, just go play out your feuds
We got no pride, don't know whose boots to lick
We act so greedy, makes me sick sick sick

"Highwire" The Rolling Stones

9

Foreign Policy and Economics

Foreign policy and economics cannot be separated. War always has a significant economic and budgetary impact attached to it. Sometimes economics is the major motivation for war. Even those wars fought for liberty have economic consequences including from wealth destruction and the interruption of markets, property rights, and trade.

Economic issues associated with wars often are related to one side seeking to gain unfair advantage over the other. Indeed, war often arises from flawed economic policies such as trade restrictions, fluctuating currency values, competitive devaluation, deliberate inflation, debt monetization, tariffs, seizures of natural resources or water access, and other issues related to corporatism and special interests.

The age-old dilemma is that so few people understand how personal liberty and free markets solve economic problems and how interventionism only makes the problems worse. The problems that have resulted from previous government intervention can hardly be solved by more of the same, and especially not by war.

Bureaucratic mischief generates new problems that lead to calls for even more political "solutions." Ultimately, a faltering economy and dependency on more government to solve the problems already generated by too much government lead to economic wars as production overall and wealth is diminished. Not surprisingly, the anger, excessive nationalism, and hostility that comes with economic war too frequently leads to a shooting war.

Inflation of the 1920s and worldwide depression of the 1930s generated the conditions, including especially currency wars, that led to the fascism of Hitler and Mussolini, while providing fuel for Lenin-inspired communism. The death and destruction that resulted as a consequence is hard to comprehend considering how harsh and grotesque things became.

Today's conditions of currency and debt chaos around the world are similar to those of the 1930s and World War II that prompted the Bretton Woods monetary system as a "solution." Though conditions are similar in the two time periods, it is my belief that the inflation and distortions that are occurring today have created problems that are far worse.

Economic failure worldwide and dependency on central bank inflation and government spending as a solution make it certain that conditions will worsen before they improve. Even with the great strides we've made in promoting free-market Austrian economics education, politics, for now, will prevent the implementation in a peaceful and deliberate fashion of the reforms required to solve our problems. The collapse of the system is probably required before the people give up their dependency on welfare solutions and government's so-called responsibility to redistribute wealth. The longer today's conditions last the more likely more major wars will break out as happened before with the Great Depression.

Another problem that hangs over the world is that there are still a lot of people who believe that war is an economic benefit and remain convinced that World War II actually ended the Great Depression. Hardly! But I've heard this too often from colleagues in Washington who should have known better and should have dismissed this thought outright. Many Americans still believe that FDR ended the Great Depression, with World War II providing a big help. The war did nothing to help, and all of FDR's economic policies, which were a continuation of Hoover's mistakes, were responsible for prolonging the depression. This same criticism can be made of the economic policies of both George W. Bush and Barack Obama that have prolonged the current Great Recession.

War spending takes butter from the dinner table

We must remember that the GDP as calculated is not an accurate measurement of real economic growth or improvement in the standard of living. Building weapons of war may benefit corporate war profiteers and highly paid union workers, but the spending is actually a negative for raising the standard of living of the average person.

The average person, who does not work in the arms industry, pays the bills and reaps no direct economic benefits from war. Middle-class Americans pay the taxes and suffer the consequences of the borrowing and the inflating of the money supply. The resulting higher prices hurt the poor and middle class more than the wealthy.

The military-industrial complex corporations never complain of higher prices for bombs, planes, drones, and missiles.

They benefit when prices rise and when cost overruns are covered with more money from the US Treasury. Those who profit are the greatest champions of the military readiness and armed conflict. They are represented by lobbyists who greatly influence both political parties. Corporate war profits and high union wages bring about remarkable cooperation between the two parties despite the political rhetoric suggesting passionate disagreement. And these militaristic policies are defended with patriotic zeal, and in appeals regarding our moral obligation to take care of all the world's needs and to meet our obligation to spread our "goodness" around the world.

The arguments against warfare fall on deaf ears with most conservatives. Too many accept the superficial arguments that Americans must have blind allegiance to militarism, that offensive war is the same as defensive war, and that war creates economic benefits.

Henry Hazlitt addressed so clearly in his classic book *Economics in One Lesson* the hidden cost of government actions. When money is spent by politicians, we must also ask where those funds would have been better spent if allowed to stay in the hands of individuals making their own choices. When we hear that the US just spent $X billion for drone missiles, we must immediately ask: "instead of what?" In other words, what else could have been achieved if that $X billion had been spent by the individuals who earned the money rather than by some nameless bureaucrat serving a powerful special interest? It should be obvious which scenario would most benefit the economy.

Spending trillions of dollars in war on bombs and missiles, planes, land vehicles, boats, buildings, infrastructure, and people means trillions of dollars denied for fulfilling people's peaceful desires. No lobbyist is there to defend the invisible victims of this system. And the irony is that the war purchases are recorded as a positive for economic growth and the GDP.

Though the war spending is an economic negative and provides no improvement in the people's standard of living, the government statisticians brag about an upward blip in the GDP. Besides, these bills are paid for by borrowing and printing money, thus increasing future debt obligations and causing higher prices for the next generation.

It's a total farce to think spending to buy military weapons that require constant replacement because they are destroyed and even frequently stolen or used against our own military is sound economic policy. It makes less sense than Paul Krugman arguing that putting more people on food stamps will help revive the economy. Useless spending that causes the fraudulent GDP to increase while increasing the national debt and inflation is not the road to prosperity. It's a highway to economic chaos.

Another downside of this type of expenditure is the enemies we create by invading, occupying, bombing, rigging elections, propping up dictators, and otherwise involving ourselves in the internal affairs of other nations and conflicts throughout the world.

All the money spent on interference in the affairs of others inevitably creates new problems for us as our enemies multiply with each act of aggression we commit. Blowback and unintended consequences are predictable. But, instead of our leaders looking at foreign policy objectively, they claim that the problems we have with the Taliban, al-Qaeda, ISIS, or another enemy demand ratcheting up our military operations. This means a greater economic drain, and a hastening of the fiscal crisis that always results from ill-advised policies that come with extending empire too far.

Replacing bad ideas with good

It's a shame that reason doesn't prevail over emotions, propaganda, and the influence of special interests. If it did, we could have put in place a noninterventionist foreign policy based on friendship, trade, property rights, and respect for others. This concept has been around for a long time. Though even our early presidents drifted from their professed beliefs, they spoke eloquently of the benefits of nonintervention.

Ideas do have consequences. Philosophy that promotes peace and harmony has been thought through. But, politicians have not allowed nonintervention policies to come to fruition. This is an argument for never granting more power to government. The frustration for those who understand the importance of ideas and their consequences is that it's often painstakingly slow to see the changes come about. Yet, educational efforts that appear to yield no policy changes for years on end can set the groundwork for quick changes in times of chaos and distress. Patience, convictions, and vigilance are required.

Freedom advanced rather slowly in the years after feudal barons forced King John to sign the Magna Carta in 1215. It took a long time before Lockean ideas helped usher in the Industrial Revolution and the American Revolution. An emphasis on the work ethic, property, and natural rights helped to bring about the magnificent changes that improved the material well-being of millions of people in a relatively short period of time.

Having peace as a goal is both a key component of sensible foreign policy and crucial to economic prosperity and equal protection of all people's liberty.

America's current crisis came about from foolish economic policies and an overreach of the empire's demands. What is needed is a new approach to foreign affairs, trade, and monetary policy. This crisis may provide a historic opportunity to witness the failure of the current system built on bad ideas and to advance a replacement consistent with the cause of liberty.

Supporting an empire that we cannot afford has sadly set us back these past 100 years. We must not forget that a nuclear exchange was not required to defeat Soviet communism. That government system defeated itself because it was based on a deeply flawed economic theory.

What ideas will rise when the US Empire falls?

The greatest political event of the 20th century was not the military victory of World War I or World War II. These wars were tragic events that would have been minimized with a better understanding and practice of the philosophy of noninterventionism by all nations in foreign affairs.

The greatest event was the acknowledgment of the failed communist monstrosity that had been tested in the Soviet Empire and cheered by many in the West, including many intellectuals and high officials in United States government like Alger Hiss and Harry Dexter White. Significant support notably came from the American economist Paul Samuelson who influenced millions of college students with his textbook Economics.

Samuelson, in 1970, was the first American to win the Nobel Prize in Economic Sciences. No doubt he had great influence on American economic and political thought—all negative. Samuelson praised the Soviet Union's economic policies and made outlandish, unfulfilled predictions. In 1973 he predicted the Soviet Union per capita income by 1990 would equal that of the United States. By 1990 the Soviet system was on its last legs.

Samuelson never gave up praising the communism that he so much admired. In his 1989 edition of Economics, just before the Berlin Wall was officially eliminated by the East Germans after weeks of civil unrest, Samuelson was still touting his affection for communism and its impending success.

Samuelson claimed in the 1989 edition of Economics that "the Soviet economy is proof that, contrary to what many skeptics had earlier believed, a socialist command economy can function and even thrive." The real tragedy is that in academic circles Samuelson has never been discredited for his analysis or his blind support for a communist regime that was responsible for the death of millions of people between 1917 and 1991. Matter of fact, economists like Paul Krugman and Ben Bernanke continue to support similar economic policies that have no more credibility for working than those of Samuelson. And, yes, I believe that they too are tenaciously clinging to ideas that will bring great havoc to America and the West, and that we're on the eve of a crushing repudiation of their failed authoritarian policies. Their presence on the current intellectual scene will prove to be about as timely as was Samuelson's defense of communism just as it was receiving its last rights.

The ideological replacement is up for grabs since the end of the current system is certain to come. A grand opportunity presents itself for true free-market principles to prevail along with a transition away from the militarism of empire to a policy of peace, friendship, and trade with all willing nations.

The replacement for the collapsed Soviet and Eastern Europe communism unfortunately was not the adoption of a free market, property rights, and sound money. Instead modified Keynesianism, corporatism, and central bank planning replaced communism. The failure of communism, which was brought down by huge foreign commitments and low production, prompted the acceptance of the Keynesian-style economic planning practiced in the West, which, at the time, was doing much better economically than the Soviet Union. The current economic system of the West faces the same threat of extinction. Out of the approaching chaos will come radical change.

Knowledge regarding economics and its relationship to foreign affairs has advanced enough that, with a sensible transition, much suffering could be avoided. But, sadly, the odds of that happening under current conditions are remote. The repeal of the Corn Laws in 1846 due in large part to the efforts of Richard Cobden and John Bright in Great Britain offers an example where repealing bad laws can prevent great suffering and turmoil. Cobden and Bright challenging the stagnating effects of mercantilism helped usher in an age of private property and free trade without economic chaos. Though such a transition is a tough goal to achieve, an effort must be made.

The soldier came knocking upon the queen's door
He said, "I am not fighting for you any more"
The queen knew she'd seen his face someplace before
And slowly she let him inside.

He said, "I've watched your palace up here on the hill
And I've wondered who's the woman for whom we all kill
But I am leaving tomorrow and you can do what you will
Only first I am asking you why."

"The Queen & The Soldier" Suzanne Vega

10

Central Bank Influence on Foreign Policy

Central banks play a significant role in foreign policy, but their role is usually ignored or not understood. Central banks are rarely neutral when it comes to financing war. Wars inevitably are paid for with borrowed money and monetary inflation. In ancient times wars were financed through plunder when taxation did not suffice. Today that is still attempted as it was in the Iraq War when we were promised that the war would be paid for by plundering the oil reserves of Iraq. That did not work out so well.

Since the inception of the Federal Reserve in 1913, the Fed has been a major player in financing war by buying government debt. If all wars were paid for through direct taxation, as they were being fought, wars would tend to be much shorter and less frequent. The convenience of government borrowing helps, but rarely suffices, to pay for war. Throughout the 20th century, inflating of the money supply by the Federal Reserve purchasing government debt with money the Fed created out of thin air was the principal source of war financing.

Wage and price controls

Governments always want to hide the fact that price increases are a direct consequence of central bank actions. That is the reason that, literally for centuries, wage and price controls were imposed to pretend to push back against "greedy workers" and "war profiteers." As far back as the fourth century AD, the Roman Emperor Diocletian imposed price controls.

Price controls always fail, causing shortages, rationing, and economic harm, along with the development of an underground or black market economy. In times of crisis, like during wars or recessions when markets are more needed than ever, wage and price controls never help and always make things worse. In a crisis it is most important that, and we should be most adamant that, the market be allowed to work.

In America wage and price controls were imposed during World War I, World War II, and the Korean War. Then, in the 1970's Nixon imposed wage and price controls during the Vietnam War, with equally devastating results. Even today, the federal and state governments, in a spotty manner, regulate prices to no avail. These market controls never help regardless of the penalties with which violators are threatened.

It's bad enough to see that so much wealth is wasted in war, along with the decrease in the standard of living for those who are not on the receiving end of war profits. The consequence of destructive economic controls, price inflation, and shortages add insult to injury.

Keynesians are adamant that war spending—or any type of government spending for that matter, even if the government prints or borrows the money—is a benefit to the economy. They could not be more wrong.

The Federal Reserve encourages and facilitates war by promising endless financing. This war financing then compounds the problems of war through debt and inflation. This is why the Federal Reserve creates a moral hazard whether the spending is for war or welfare.

The path to war

Even before a war starts the central bank helps create economic conditions that significantly contribute to hostilities: boom and bust cycles, recessions, depressions, competitive devaluations, and trade wars can be laid at the feet of the Federal Reserve officials and, in particular, the chairman or chairwoman of the Fed as the person with the most influence.

As economic conditions deteriorate and production decreases during a business downturn, wealth decreases and a lower standard of living for the middle class and poor results, causing conflicts to arise. Domestically the wealthy are enriched with such a system. Internationally, debt burdens and currency wars undermine international trade, aggravating relationships with other nations. Political pressure prompts protectionist measures, including tariffs and any other policy actions that can help distract from the true cause of the problems. Domestically, the rich are blamed; internationally, other nations are blamed for using "unfair trade policies." This unstable economic environment manufactured by the Fed and other central banks is all too often conducive for military conflict.

The evidence of this sequence of events stares one in the face if one looks objectively at the events of the 20th century. First we got the Fed, then the inflation for World War I followed, and then the predictable 1921 Depression arrived. That was only a warm-up for the Fed inflation of 1920s, the Great Depression of the 1930s, trade and currency wars, and Germany's ruinous inflation. As anticipated by many, we next had World War II. It should have surprised no one.

The process has continued. No more "depressions" though; that word has been mothballed. Now we have only "great" recessions. This puts us back to repeating history. In many ways today's conditions are similar to those before World War II but much more dangerous for the US. The US is the greatest debtor nation ever, and the monetary expansion worldwide is the greatest of all history, led by the Federal Reserve thanks to Alan Greenspan, Ben Bernanke, and Janet Yellen.

Central banking and foreign policy cannot be separated.

Opportunity in the dollar collapse

The wars, even though a major cause of the mess, continue, and Keynesian silliness is persistently followed in Washington. Spend, spend, spend, deficits, deficits, deficits, borrow, borrow, borrow, print, print, print, but do not succumb to seeking or accepting the truth of the calamity that is being manufactured by our monetary and political leaders. The truth is obvious. Yet, the decision makers remain in total denial or ignorance.

So the Fed financed wars to satisfy special interests and having nothing to do with national security proceed unabated. But that will end in time as the dollar system unravels. Then there will be a great opportunity—if our educational effort has been successful in creating enough widespread understanding of the freedom philosophy to rebuild and advance the cause of liberty. While it must be realized that there will always be those seeking wars of aggression, a sound monetary policy coupled with the absence of a central bank would go a long way in diminishing the ability of the warmongers to pursue military operations.

The question I am often asked is "why?" Why do our political and intellectual leaders continue policies that defy common sense? My assessment is that it's probably a combination of many reasons.

Some people driving US foreign policy sincerely believe that, because of our dominant position in the world, we have a moral obligation to intervene for humanitarian reasons. There are also those who support intervention for much less noble reasons—oil, power, military-industrial complex profits, etc.—and take advantage of the sentiment of the right and left supporters who want to solve problems such as border disputes and chaotic civil unrest within other countries.

There are yet others who thrive on chaos and endless wars they see as creating opportunities to remake the world. Some "world remakers" will even go so far as to engineer false flag incidents to help justify war to the people. They will also take advantage to escalate hostilities when blowback and unintended consequences occur and use jingoistic propaganda to support even more war and spending.

Our government school system, increasingly an arm of the federal government, has negatively influenced many generations of Americans and especially those now running our federal government, making them more amenable to supporting war.

Bad economic policy has provided a major boost to the perpetuation of authoritarian, aggressive foreign policy. Monetary policy has facilitated the finance of all wars since the US entered World War I in 1917, four years after the Fed was established. But the full influence of monetary policy on foreign affairs is much more pervasive and secretive. This became evident from the trillions of dollars of bailouts during the financial crisis of 2008 and 2009. In secret the Fed was able to churn trillions of dollars through the world banking system, not only in America but also in Europe and other parts of the world.

Banking is now global in nature so the bailing out a large bank or corporation has international significance. Many of the funds were even used to directly assist particular countries and other central banks. The effort to do so obviously made little sense for the dollar long term. But, it was said to be in everyone's interest to paper over the crisis and protect the banking system in the short term.

During the several decades that I worked on exposing the Fed for all the harm it causes, the information it was most protective of was its foreign operations. Even with the revelations that due to congressional pressure were finally made after the onset of the recent crisis, the Fed never fully explained how the trillions of dollars used to bail out foreign entities, international banks, and foreign countries were actually used. Further, the fact that all this financial activity occurred outside the view of a sleeping Congress is astounding and frightening. The day must come when this power is reined in. Unfortunately, it's not likely to happen before a dollar crisis of major proportion occurs.

Although much was learned through congressional inquiry about the massive, secret bailouts, much information is still not available to the people or to the Congress. The secrecy of the Federal Reserve regarding these bailouts begs the question: How active is the Fed in propping up foreign governments, helping war efforts, and secretly funding foreign elections and military coups around the world? There's no way to know how much has occurred in the past or is still happening. Considering the US government's politically-motivated IRS actions, CIA torture programs, NSA mass surveillance, and other scandals, nothing should surprise us. Big government is out of control.

The problem of loans, supported by unlimited credit coming out of a Fed computer, that can be used for political and military operations—all outside the appropriation process and oversight of Congress—needs a close assessment. Also, the massive interference in the currency and bond markets in recent years deserves scrutiny. The Fed buys plenty of US debt with newly created credit, but so do other countries. It's quite possible that the credit can literally come from the Fed with a quid pro quo that those who receive it—banks or other countries—then buy Treasury bills to continue the fraudulent system designed to provide false confidence in the dollar as a reserve currency. And it is quite likely that our government and/or the Fed interferes in the gold market to suppress gold's dollar price in an effort to support the dollar on international exchange markets.

US bankers today can get "free" dollars at will and can use them to purchase US debt, keep rates low, and boost the dollar all while earning interest on their excess reserves that the Fed generated. It's a con game that cannot last. There will come a day when it's not in the interest of other nations to finance our debt no matter how they get their dollars. These easy loans certainly have not been used to rebuild the American economy. Instead they have given life to the reemergence of a stock bubble, rising prices of houses once again, and a continuation of the bond bubble. But, eventually the markets will rule and force a readjustment. Our trade imbalance and our huge current account deficits prompt foreign holders of dollars and US debt to prop up the system in their own interests. But one should be prepared for the day when their incentive to acquire and hold US dollars disappears. When that happens, the world changes. That process may have already started.

Free market advocates rightfully target the Federal Reserve for the economic harm it causes. More people every day are waking up to the fact that the Fed is guilty of creating the economic chaos and that it is unable to rescue us from the dangers that are supposedly caused by the free market.

It's not widely known how the Federal Reserve can and has gotten involved in foreign policy through the use of credit in secret. The Fed is constantly involved in the freezing of financial assets of uncooperative nations when directed by Congress, the Treasury, or executive order. What the Fed does at its own discretion and without permission or oversight by the Congress in times of war and peace to help or hurt friends or enemies should also be exposed and prohibited.

A policy to achieve peace and prosperity will never be fully realized so long as there is a central bank with secretive power to issue, at will, a fiat currency and to engage in central economic planning by manipulating the market and interest rates and providing benefits to friends. This interference in the financial markets generates so much disequilibrium and distortion. It creates international frictions that frequently lead to war.

There are always economic issues involved in war no matter what other issues the people may be concentrating on as a result of propaganda. And these economic issues are strong motivating factors that drive nations to war. The US record for peace since 1913 is, to say the least, dismal. Much of the blame should be laid at the feet of our central bank and its partners in crime.

It should not be a surprise to find that the strongest proponents for peace—and thus prosperity—are strongly opposed to the Federal Reserve and central banking. The power to create money out of thin air is so great that it should never be given to the politicians and secretive central bankers. That power will always be abused as the individuals in charge yield to the temptation for legalized counterfeiting in which they can engage. A commodity currency that arises from market forces and without fraud is the monetary system that would give each nation the best chance of working toward peaceful relations.

Fathers are pleading, lovers are all alone
Mothers are praying—send our sons back home
You marched them away—yes, you did—on ships and planes
To the senseless war, facing death in vain
"Bring the Boys Home" Freda Payne

11

A Unilateral Declaration of Peace

Some will argue that, unless all nations in the world uniformly announce their support for and initiate nonintervention in foreign affairs, sound money without central banks, and free trade, then a transition toward peace, freedom, and prosperity can't work and shouldn't be tried. That, however, is an excuse for the authoritarians to continue to exert their power over all things political and economic.

Fiat money is a government power it is important to challenge. Matter of fact, government management of money has been implemented worldwide with nothing to show for it except an exacerbation of the problems politicians claimed they were going to prevent.

The world gave up on the international gold standard—managed by no one country or group of countries—in 1914. This transition ushered in a century of economic chaos and constant wars. The world tried a politically-driven gold-exchange standard starting in 1945. That attempted fix was followed by the absolutely no gold standard after 1971. Both systems failed. Today the world is enmeshed in war and an economic system that rewards the military-industrial complex, the international banks, and the privileged corporations. Constant and excessive growth of government is also fueled.

World War I, the supposed noble war to "end all wars" and make the world "safe for democracy," gave us the Treaty of Versailles that subsequently caused the world to engage in multiple wars. The artificial national boundaries that the treaty dictated, especially in the Middle East, continue to lead to wars. World War II was a consequence of World War I and the continuation of flawed economic and foreign policies. Even though the League of Nations experiment with global government failed after World War I, the authoritarians proceeded to expand global government with the United Nations, the IMF, the World Bank, and the WTO, principally controlled by the current empire of note—the United States. Though the powerbrokers have not yet been willing to admit failure, this approach will be seen as creating more problems than it has solved, considering the conflict, turmoil, and economic crisis of the world today.

If world government doesn't work, must we assume that a single country is ill-advised to go it alone with sound money, nonintervention in foreign affairs, and free trade? The people worldwide have been indoctrinated that there must instead be official political agreements among nations bringing them together in world government. This widely held perception greatly benefits the wealthy powerbrokers.

Given that central banks and intervention through international agreements, alliances, and organizations have failed to support peace, freedom, and prosperity for a hundred years and have actually made things worse, shouldn't we replace that approach with something proven to yield good results? International trade worked rather well from 1875 to 1914 with a gold standard and comparatively noninterventionist government. Many agreements were voluntary, nonpolitical, and market-based among countries without any international government interfering. Instead of improving on this system, it was rejected outright, and the world's chances for peace and prosperity were undermined.

A nation can unilaterally adhere to a policy of nonintervention in the affairs of other nations and benefit from it. It is not necessary to have nations combining into larger entities with the goal of achieving world government. War is costly in so many ways; but peace is economically beneficial. Peace allows more wealth to go to the people instead of to death, destruction, civil liberties violations, and profits for the warmongers. And a country can adopt good policies on its own whether it's a large or small country. Others will follow when the benefits are seen. An official agreement among nations prior to the implementation of noninterventionist policies is not usually feasible and is never necessary. Giving power to an international government leads only to competition in power struggles and international conflicts.

What about the danger to a country if it decides to avoid entangling alliances and constant interference in the affairs of other countries? Some argue that to be safe and have trade with others requires international treaties, military alliances, monetary coordination, and government-managed trade. Ardent advocacy for global management usually comes from the economically strong countries with the strongest trade balances, creditor nations with a strong currency and military. For the last 100 years it's been the British and Americans who have dictated policy. Soon it's likely to be the Chinese.

This history does not rule out any one nation standing alone on policy. Switzerland has done rather well with its streak of independence. Reasonable fiscal and monetary policy, along with the rejection of foreign intervention, have been beneficial to her. Switzerland did not suffer militarily from her independence. Two world wars were fought in Switzerland's neighborhood, and yet her wealth and independence were maintained.

A country that follows its own policies of free markets, sound money, free trade, and a strategic military independence will become safer and richer for it. The obsession with neomercantilism and empire building, which the US has had for way too long, should be rejected.

Look at the mess we're in with an $18 trillion national debt ($6 trillion owed to other nations) and troops in over 140 countries. This is supposedly all done for the protection of our "national security interests." What a hoax! China, which has not been placing troops all over the world, is putting surplus cash in investments around the world with no loss of life while becoming wealthier with economic growth. Meanwhile, our middle class shrinks and grows poorer and our businesses leave our shores. Blaming others—especially the Chinese—for our plight and the challenge to dollar hegemony will not reverse the course on which the US is traveling. To reverse course, we must undergo a self-assessment and a change in our policies. The opportunity is coming with the growing failure of our obsession with interventionism.

It is generally believed that a policy of free trade has to be multinational and managed by an international government agency and its bureaucrats. This sounds logical to some. But, as always, any good intentions of economic planners give way to the authoritarian opportunists. They end up running the intergovernmental agencies to serve special interests and particular nations. This "regulatory capture" is true for international bureaucracy just as it is for domestic bureaucracy.

Free trade should be instituted for the benefit of the country that desires it, whether others agree to it or not. The populists and protectionists argue that free trade would destroy the domestic economy and that everyone else who does not follow free trade would take advantage of the free trade country by selling products to it cheaper due the absence of import tariffs and other protectionist measures. It is true that the more countries that engage in free trade and sound monetary policies the better it would be for the world economy. But legislating through international governmental bodies will not create the conditions desired since the matter will become a political football and the special interests will win.

It is of course better when many nations voluntarily follow free-trade practices. This more optimal possibility, however, should not prevent a country from unilaterally following free-trade principles for its own benefit.

Countries that continue to subsidize their exports, as most countries competitively do today (including through currency manipulation), become poorer. A free-trade country would become richer by importing goods that are cheaper due to foreign subsidies. The money saved can be spent on other items to improve the overall wealth in the country.

Any country that is determined to invoke free-trade principles should also be supportive of low taxes, less regulations, and sound money. Eliminating the threat of central bank-induced business cycle ups and downs would be a major benefit that would help the country to remain competitive. If a country ever took these steps on its own, the beneficial results would encourage others to follow.

Though free trade may be entered into solely for its economic benefits, this environment of trade and friendship with other countries, with all sides benefiting, encourages peaceful relations among nations, thus reducing the chance of war.

Trade problems and imbalances of payments significantly contribute to the resentments that frequently lead to war.

Free trade is very different from the policies the world follows today. The so-called free traders in Washington who preach support for NAFTA, the WTO, the IMF, and various international "free-trade agreements" are often also the ones who constantly call for sanctions on countries they want to dominate for various political and economic reasons. Supporters of these so-called free-trade agreements are disingenuous since the agreements are nothing more than rules for managed trade that benefit large special interests.

Sanctions are an economic policy that hinders wealth creation, liberty, and peace. And, besides, sanctions don't work. We eventually end up hurting ourselves as much as the recipients of our sanctions. Indeed, an opposed nation's political leaders can often rally domestic support by blaming sanctions for people's troubles. Too frequently, it is these sanctioned countries we end up fighting. Sanctions didn't work on Japan, Iraq, Iran, Cuba, and other nations. They are economically dangerous and a principal cause of war.

A country unilaterally can, to its own advantage, adhere to free trade, commodity money, and noninterventionism in all foreign affairs. The results would be a richer and safer country with a lot more friends around the world and a radically reduced propensity to engage in military conflict. War for a country that followed these rules would only be defensive in nature, when it was attacked by another nation. And, for the US, engaging in war should require a congressional declaration of war—something we have not seen since World War II.

Progress will be made when the people demand a more sensible foreign policy and fewer wars. The only question remaining is this: When will the American people gain enough self-confidence, economic knowledge, and common sense to demand that our political leaders come to their senses for the sake of ensuring peace and prosperity for the people?

Free trade and leniency in international travel is beneficial to everyone. This policy challenges those who would resort to wage limits by government controls and the artificially high wages resulting from government-derived powers exercised by labor unions. Even with strict controls on labor moving from one country to another, companies seek out lower wages by moving their businesses to those countries where labor is provided at more competitive levels. When labor is allowed to freely move and seek out opportunities anywhere in the world, workers can make the most money possible and have greater access to jobs. If market rules prevail, the productivity of workers, instead of the dictates of bureaucrats and politicians, will determine wages. While it is true that wages may come down at times if this were to happen, those affected individuals would then have a much lower cost of living and be rewarded for increasing production. If an artificially high wage of $20 drops to $15 and the job is guaranteed that's a better deal than having a wage of $20 or $25 but no work when the business moves overseas to seek more competitive wages or is put out of business. Under a free-market system prices not only would not rise significantly, they would probably fall. When wages are kept artificially high by government rules and inflation, the worker's standard of living falls. Real wages rise under free trade.

If labor and capital cannot freely come into a country or leave, jobs will (freely) go out. Then the temptation will be to use physical walls, barbwire fences, and currency controls to prevent the adjustments that efficient markets demand. Prosperity is enhanced for all concerned when labor and capital move freely across borders without political interference. And so is peace!

It is a false assumption that a free-trade system would hurt workers. Today's system is what is destroying the middle class wage earner. Jobs are less available, and the cost of living is skyrocketing. The welfare-warfare system is destructive to the prosperity of the poor and middle class. It instead serves the interests of the powerful and rich who reap the benefits of the inflation, the military-industrial complex, spending, and bail-outs. A sensible foreign policy of nonintervention should include the freedom to travel to wherever work is available and wherever there is a demand. There should never be a promise of welfare for those people who are unwilling to travel to find work. For too long we've been taught that such a system would hurt the working class. The opposite is true.

But every time I read the papers,
That old feeling comes on.
We're waist deep in the Big Muddy
And the big fool says to push on.

"Waist Deep in the Big Muddy" Pete Seeger

12

Strong Leaders and Foreign Affairs

There are two sides to human nature. I'm not talking about the ancient conflict between good and evil, which all societies have had to deal with. I'm talking about another conflict that has been around for a long time as well—the desire for liberty and self-reliance versus governments that promise safety and economic well-being.

Those who seek security first and foremost are susceptible to the promises of strong leaders boasting and exerting power.

Those individuals who are insecure and naive are always tempted by the political promises and are very susceptible to the rhetoric of a "strong, charismatic leader."

A majority that yields to the promises of security instead of seeking liberty and self-reliance is giving up something real and valuable in return for false promises. The fact that strong leaders are willing to demagogue, spin, deceive, and lie proves their goal is neither to care for the people nor to advance liberty. Instead, it's their perverted desire to rule over others that drives them. But, even authoritarian regimes don't last if there isn't general acceptance of their governance by the people.

Honest concern for the people's wellbeing, that is, for peace and prosperity, would direct curiosity into understanding why policies that protect liberty and peace are far superior to anything that a "strong leader" in authoritarian and dictatorial fashion could ever provide.

Refuting the false promises requires philosophic understanding of economic interventionism, central banking, and the deeply flawed foreign policy of meddling in the affairs of other nations.

Wartime presidents are especially attractive to those individuals who lack confidence in the benefits of a free society. Unfortunately our government school system promotes big government and is a reason that for generations children have been taught that our best and strongest presidents are wartime presidents. Some of our presidents actually looked forward to managing a war in order to secure for themselves recognition in history as "strong leaders."

Presidents who "take charge" against any perceived threats that generate fear in the people are well received. Those presidents whose goal is to run things and who believe the people are incapable of running their own lives will deliberately build up fear to obtain compliance from the people as the people's liberty is taken away.

Currently we're suffering from the fear instilled into Americans that another 9/11 is just around the corner. We've also been brainwashed into believing the Federal Reserve just saved us from a total financial collapse in the past seven years even though the Fed was one of the most important causes of the crisis. To deal with the threats of another attack and another financial crisis we are expected to complacently accept endless spending, endless debt, endless bailouts, endless inflation by the Federal Reserve, endless spending by the Congress, and even endless war.

Too many people still believe it was only big government and a strong leader that got us out of the Great Depression by massively increasing the size and scope of the US government. Likewise, we're supposed to believe that World War II was an economic benefit that played a significant role in finally ending the depression. Neither belief could be further from the truth.

Most Americans believe that FDR was one of the best US presidents ever. His strong leadership was instrumental to his political success. Few people question exactly how this strength was supposedly used for the betterment of the people.

The American people have been repeatedly told that a "strong leader" is equated with authoritarian use of power to undermine liberty. Instead of valuing the demonstration of strong character in resisting the use of power, a strong president is said to be one who takes advantage of the people's emotions and their desires to be taken care of. Whether the policies actually work or not is rarely considered. The problems confronted are even oftentimes concocted or caused by earlier government actions.

What is forgotten is that a politician exercises real strength when he has access to power and an open invitation to satisfy his own ego by coming to the rescue of the people begging to be made safe and secure, yet resists the temptation. Real strength is required for leaders to resist this temptation to dominate others, and to instead act to secure liberty for the people and coming generations.

Instead of accepting the assessment of the government schools telling us who the strong and, thus, the great presidents are, we should look elsewhere for guidance. A good place to start is to read the book *Recarving Rushmore* by Ivan Eland. In the book, Eland ranks our presidents in quite a different manner. He ranks them on the basis of their support for peace, prosperity, and liberty. Those presidents who he ranks high have generally been thought to be weak or totally irrelevant. Yet, only a person of strong character and will can resist the demands of the special interests for war, spending, welfare, inflation, and restraints on liberty.

The conventional wisdom is that only a president who uses the power of the state to rule over others is a strong leader. Could it not be that a strong leader is the one who resists using government force and who instead uses his energy to consistently defend the Constitution and the cause of liberty?

So they collected the cripples, the wounded, the maimed
And they shipped us back home to Australia
The armless, the legless, the blind, the insane
Those proud wounded heroes of Suvla
And as our ship pulled into Circular Quay
I looked at the place where my legs used to be
And thank Christ there was nobody waiting for me
To grieve and to mourn and to pity
And the band played Waltzing Matilda
As they carried us down the gangway
But nobody cheered, they just stood and stared
Then turned all their faces away

"And the Band Played Waltzing Matilda" The Pogues

13

War Clichés, Miscalculations, and Tragic Consequences

The bad results of war are endless. Many come as unintended consequences and in retaliation for needlessly entering a war under false pretense. Miscalculations regarding the intent and determination of the enemy is commonplace, especially if an attack is responded to by people defending their homeland. These defenders are inspired beyond all expectations, and the aggressors have difficulty comprehending the defenders' ability to achieve victory over much more powerful forces.

So many misconceptions, so many lies, so many excuses, so much fearmongering, and so many special interests involved. Obfuscations par excellence. It's all used to gain public acceptance for starting wars. It's used to maintain support for the wars and find the cannon fodder and the funds to pay for the insanities of war. The people are tired of it and want to hear the truth.

Some of the clichés, the miscalculations, and the tragic consequences of war follow.

War wounded as political props

Once a war is underway the process of deceit continues with regard to the troops who return with broken bodies and broken minds, especially when the wars were never justified. Admitting that the wars are senseless and in vain is too much to bear.

The efforts, by many, to care for the maimed are well-meaning but often fall far short of rehabilitating the suffering individuals back into a normal life. Efforts to take care of the wounded troops returning are promoted with publicity and pomp, while placing the wounded on pedestals of heroism and calling them great patriots as if that would help heal their wounds. It is tragic to see the wounded being used as political props. This must be done to satisfy the subconscious guilt of those who supported the war and are morally responsible for all the suffering. Without this, the promoters and instigators of aggressive wars would experience the guilt that would come with facing the truth. Few ever admit their errors in judgment nor lament their actions that brought death, destruction, and heartache.

The "blame America first crowd"

The war propagandists' first retort to a war critic is to declare that that person is part of the "blame America first crowd." The proponents of war pretend that only they know right from wrong and that when they declare a necessity for war anyone who objects is wrong and un-American. This is especially the case when US foreign policy errors create so much hatred and desire for retaliation. When an explanation of how our policies backfire on us cannot be refuted, the war proponents accuse their critics of just blaming America, rather than our "hated enemies" who want to kill us in retaliation for our aggression.

Any objection to war is said to be showing sympathy for America's enemies. Blind support for the state's war is required with no dissent whatsoever acceptable. Since early in our history, unfortunately, popular opinion supported the government over the critics of war. This has been the case from the time of the Alien and Sedition Acts of 1798 under John Adams to the current PATRIOT Act, NSA surveillance, and the FISA court. And, all along, almost all our wartime presidents—Lincoln, Wilson, FDR, George W. Bush, and Obama to name a few— have abused war dissenters.

The message has always been loud and clear: In time of war there will be no dissent; the government is right; anyone disagreeing is un-American; criticism of the war effort means one is just blaming America and therefore cannot be patriotic regardless of the circumstance of the war.

Critics become criminals since truth is anathema to an empire or any authoritarian government that depends on lies for its existence. The informant who provides the people with the truth cannot be protected by whistle-blower laws or the Constitution. It is the truth-tellers who are sent to prison or are killed while those who undermine our Constitution are promoted. This lasts until the corrupt government is dismantled.

The peril of entangling alliances

It may sound like a good idea to participate in multilateral defense agreements and become involved in the internal affairs of other nations "to protect our national security interests," but there is no evidence to suggest this is a wise move for any country.

We were advised early in our history by the Founders that it would be best to avoid entangling alliances and interference in the internal affairs of other nations. Instead they advised us to offer friendship and trade with all countries for our own self-interest. This is an uncomplicated foreign policy. Simply stated, we ought to mind our own business, work on our own imperfections, and, if we desire to spread the message of liberty, do so by setting an example while rejecting any temptation to force our views and ways on others.

This advice was specifically directed at staying out of constant struggles and violence in Europe. That advice would still serve us well; we ought to militarily leave Europe completely. Additionally, the advice should promptly be followed to end the obsession we have with our entanglements and military presence in the Middle East. And the sooner the better! To compound problems, the US is now also moving towards greater intervention in Asia and Africa.

Since World War II we have become more involved throughout the world under the umbrella of international organizations including NATO and the United Nations. These are mere vehicles for facilitating our presence overseas while avoiding congressional supervision, including the constitutional requirement of obtaining a congressional declaration of war for our military operations. Our money controls these organizations, and Congress never resists appropriating the funds requested, being easily convinced that it's in our national security interest. The Founders would be shocked by and disappointed with the current US foreign policy of expansive commitments throughout the world.

Fear and hate

Without fear and hate directed toward an enemy there would be no war. Fear and hate comes from the propaganda of the war proponents that is always couched in terms of "defense" and protecting national security. Almost all the major media accommodate the propagandists in these efforts. People naturally desire to love their country and believe it can do no harm. The problem arises when there's confusion between one's country and a government that professes to speak for the people and its entire culture but in reality serves the special interests.

To accept the warmongers' demands, the people must reject their natural desire for peace and prosperity over war and impoverishment. For war proponents to achieve this change in thought—something governments have been able to do since ancient times—the people must be convinced they are indeed threatened if war is not pursued. Fear of an enemy is required whether the threat is real or not. And the danger has to be thought to be imminent.

So far it's been difficult to build an emotional case for war against Iran over a weapon she does not possess. But the American people came to believe after a year and a half of war propaganda that Saddam Hussein was on the verge of launching an attack on America at any moment using his stockpile of weapons of mass destruction that did not exist. Scott Ritter, the UN's weapons inspector, made an effort to get the truth out before the war. He was met with a concerted effort to destroy his credibility. It may take time, but the people must experience fear to become proponents of war. Our government officials, along with their media and special interest allies, are expert at prompting that fear.

The war propaganda effort requires demonizing the enemy, especially the leader of the country targeted. It's easier to convince people to sacrifice to fight another "Hitler" than an enemy who demonstrates an element of humanity. That is the role of the propagandists: Demonize and build hate regardless of how many lies have to be told.

None of this works unless it's done in the name of patriotism. Those individuals who refuse to join in the lies supporting the war are condemned as being unpatriotic, ill-informed, or friends of the enemy. If the propaganda doesn't silence them and they are seen as a sufficient threat to the war machine, the government will enact laws granting power to arrest and punish those refusing to succumb to the propaganda. This will be done not only to punish the direct targets. It will also be done to frighten others who may be considering boldly challenging the authoritarians supporting a war that will only benefit the special interests.

Sadly this process started early in our history with Adams's Alien and Sedition Acts in 1798 and has continued through our history to the present day with Obama reinvigorating the Espionage Act of 1917.

Hermann Goering claimed that the process of getting the people to support war, and to die in and pay for war, was the same in any political system. Because human nature was the same, according to Goering, the propaganda worked whether it was used in a democracy or a fascist or communist dictatorship. Publicizing a threat of danger, even when made up, and exciting patriotic zeal are tactics of the propagandists.

To overcome the lies governments tell, we must seek truth. What is required is knowledge and a belief in a moral principle that rejects the wars the government starts for the benefit of the powerful few at the expense of the people.

Blowback

Blowback is considered an unintended consequence of aggression, but all unintended consequences are not considered to be blowback. When our policies surprisingly come back to haunt us militarily it's called blowback. Even if providing motivation for blowback is unintended, it is certainly not unforeseen by people who have studied US interventions and their repercussions.

Authors including Chalmers Johnson and Michael Scheuer have written extensively about the significance of the concept of blowback. Blowback is a term coined by the CIA. Promoters of aggression, like the neoconservatives, either deny blowback exists or refuse to accept that their effort to remake the world to their desires may cause blowback.

It's understandable that the concept of blowback has to be either ignored or refuted by war propagandists. Blowback indicates that the policies pursued by our government are deeply flawed and that the cost is much higher than the war promoters admit.

One reason that blowback deniers get away with not being blamed is that a blowback incident may take years to occur in reaction to the interference or aggression by outside forces. An example is the overthrow of the Iranian Shah in 1979. This occurred after the radicalization of some Islamists whose anger had been building since the United States and Britain in 1953 overthrew the democratically elected Iranian leader Mohammad Mosaddegh. The hatred and hostility between United States and Iranian governments has continued since.

The 9/11 attack on America is a clear example of blowback as a consequence of US policy in the Middle East. Osama bin Laden was quite pleased with the attack. Whether he was the chief planner or not, bin Laden explained there were three reasons for the 9/11 terrorist attack. First: the constant bombing of Iraq and the hundreds of thousands of children that died as a consequence of our sanctions on that country. Second: placing troops on the Arabian Peninsula, a place considered holy land by Muslims. And third: the apparent bias he saw against the Palestinians and in favor of Israel by the US.

It seems that the longer the resentment smolders due to our presence, interference, and domination in a foreign land, the greater the rage becomes against us. The risk of a blowback incident grows the longer such intervention continues.

As I write, the US still can dominate and intimidate almost any nation of the world with threats of military force or grants or denials of funds, weapons, or favorable trade policies. Most nations generally acquiesce to US demands. But the stage is set for attacks against us either in the form of terrorism or ganging up on us once our economy gets hit and our military is seen as a paper tiger.

Anger will build as the hypocrisy of US policies becomes more obvious. The US spies, bombs, and occupies and then turns around and condemns others for doing the very same thing. We pretend our innocence and brag of our "exceptionalism," but when whistle-blowers tell the truth about our policies, the heavy hand of the state comes down on them because the state's cover is blown. Blowback danger will be with us for a long time unless we change our ways.

Bin Laden stated his goal was for the US to bankrupt itself by fighting a war without end as he had helped achieve with the Soviets, ironically with our help, in Afghanistan in the 1980s. He claimed that, by enticing us into war, it would be easier to kill Americans. Nearly 3,000 people were killed in America on 9/11. Then, the Islamists "paid" for it by the sacrifice of over 6,800 US troops plus likely as many private contractors dying and trillions of dollars spent in wars in Afghanistan and Iraq.

The bankruptcy that bin Laden desired is at our doorstep. His goal of causing great dissent within the United States over war as arose during the Vietnam War, though, did not occur as he had hoped. Apathy in America toward the death and destruction of our wars in the Middle East stifled public expression of outrage. And, except for a few members, Congress never significantly resisted the presidents, Republican or Democrat, who expanded our military activities overseas. There are some signs that this may be changing with the American people having strongly opposed Obama's plan to bomb Syria in 2013.

Something else happened too. Our own government systematically started to undermine liberty at home. Many Americans became obsessed with safety and lost their desire and love for liberty. This attitude allowed our government to do to us what bin Laden was incapable of doing and no other nation ever could do, i.e., destroy our liberty with the complicity of the people and the Congress. And sadly this process continues as our foreign policy stays the same. Not only do we remain in danger of another 9/11 type of attack, our liberties continue to be undermined by our government.

It's sad but true that the pain, suffering, and costs go on. Today, with 22 American military veterans committing suicide each day, it's impossible to claim any victory from our decades of misadventure in the wars that our leaders have dragged us into. Much of this could have been prevented with a simple understanding of the significance of blowback arising from our ridiculous obsession of maintaining a military presence around the world and fighting no-win, unconstitutional wars. Not being able to morally justify our wars contributes significantly to the suffering of our veterans.

The bad results in Iraq and Afghanistan will continue to be a burden to us for a long time. Yet there seems to be little hesitation to continue to expand our military involvement around the world. There is now a consensus of many or our political leaders to make military plans to confront our "banker" and trading partner China. Russia is also targeted.

One can only imagine what a different kind of foreign policy we would have if our political leaders understood blowback and were honestly concerned about peace and prosperity for the American people. A foreign policy based on the Golden Rule would be a good place to start.

When we reach a time, which is inevitable, when we can no longer pay the bills for maintaining and expanding our empire, we then can hopefully protect our liberty and recognize the important difference between a republican form of government and an empire once again. Cicero tried to explain the difference in the waning years of the Roman Republic a long time ago and lost his head over it. We can do better this time around.

War turns out worse than expected

Most everything that happens after hostilities break out in a war is unintended. Misconceptions are numerous. Events are unpredictable. Costs are underestimated. Paying for the war is never as easy as planned—remember the promise that oil revenues would pay for the Iraq War. The wars generally last longer than anticipated. Weaker countries like Afghanistan, due to their claim of the moral high ground since they are fighting to expel foreign invaders, do astoundingly well, with so much less. Powers like the United States and the Soviets were defeated after their invasions of Afghanistan. And there are quite a few other examples throughout history, including our disastrous experience in Vietnam.

Resilience of the people whose country is invaded is never accurately measured before a war. This leads to prolonging death and destruction on both sides. The US in the 1960s foolishly entered into the Vietnam civil war on the side of those who opposed Ho Chi Minh. US military action began with a few hundred special forces troops training south Vietnamese soldiers in 1961. We stayed for 12 years and lost—badly. The Vietnam War in the 1960s and the early '70s led to constant unrest in the United States.

During the Vietnam War, the United States government dropped seven million tons of bombs on Vietnam—a country about the size of New Mexico. This was more than twice the bombs the US used in all of World War II. What a price we paid for nothing. What a waste. What a lack of intelligence of those individuals that the American people permitted to be in leadership positions and to pursue this senseless war without any concern about the rule of law, the Constitution, and a little common sense. This is an insult to the intelligence of the human race—astounding!

The greatest danger of the wars that are intended to be limited and short is that they morph into something huge, horrible, and incomprehensible like World War I. This "war to end all wars" and our unnecessary participation in it set the stage for a century of carnage unlike anything mankind had ever experienced.

We have seen a lot of small wars, in comparison to World War I and World War II, in the 21st century. Many of these more recent wars have been costly and prolonged, with results never what was promised by the instigators of the wars. But none of these wars has engulfed the world as did those two major wars in the 20th century. This does not, however, mean that relative containment is easily achieved or that the more limited wars of the 21st century should be dismissed as less dangerous.

The danger remains that the killing of US citizens, whether by accident, plan, or a false flag incident, could fuel a massive expansion of a small war going on today. Our many involvements around the world are an open invitation for such an attack. The longer we stay in the Middle East and aggravate the problems in that region, the greater the danger of war spreading. The region is a powder keg, and our presence there only continues to stir up trouble. That Russia, China, and Iran have great interest and presence in the region adds to the complications that might arise. An event involving one of these nations could easily bring on an escalation of hostilities that no one has yet anticipated.

In the fields the bodies burning
As the war machine keeps turning

"War Pigs" Black Sabbath

14

Drone Warfare

We now have a novelty for the promoters of war: drone warfare. It may seem like war games, but it is real war.

Modern drone technology has provided what is seen as a modern form of war, different from the old-fashioned invasion and occupation to control America's conquered subjects. But, drone attacks still provide the ability to kill supposed enemies. This new technology is appealing to the authoritarians who argue that using drones is less violent and cheaper while exposing US military personnel to less danger. President Obama is a big fan.

In the age of video games, sterile and distant targeted killing of only the "bad guys" may seem like an attractive improvement in how to conduct war and kill anyone who plots to undermine US plans and actions around the world. Not actually being near the enemy is also supposed to help the weapons operators to psychologically adjust to aggression without remorse.

Drone warfare occurs with even less congressional oversight than we've had over warfare for the past fifty-plus years. This allows the wars to be controlled by civilians in secret through the operation of the NSA and the CIA. And of course it's meant to be more attractive because of greatly reducing casualties, that is for American soldiers. People in the countries being targeted, however, never seem to be of much concern to our political leaders. Before it's all over for us as an empire, drone strikes will motivate and inspire a determined and expansive enemy more likely to retaliate with terrorist attacks than by conventional means.

It will turn out that drone killing will be resented every bit as much as old-fashioned bombing, invasion, and occupation. The fact that the killing comes in such a stealth manner, where the operators are thousands of miles away and never show their faces, incites hatred just as much as or more than conventional warfare.

Drone targeting often depends on identification on the ground by informants and enemies of those targeted. Targets are identified for reasons related to revenge and disputes between competing foreign groups. The US ends up doing the dirty work in feuds. Locating an individual for targeted killing may also be accomplished by means including placing electronic devices on certain people or cars or tracking a cell phone. Though this process seems simple, it still requires numerous people to operate the whole program, and actually more individuals are used in this manner than are involved in a bombing run by a jet aircraft.

Mistakes are frequently made. This has occurred with drone attacks on weddings and funerals. The US sometimes pays money to families for the mistakes and expects all to be forgiven and forgotten. But, things don't work out that way; the killings are remembered and hatred grows. Many days of payback await us.

We shouldn't be surprised if blowback incidents continue, especially overseas. And most likely they will occur here at home as well. Continuing and expanding the Global War on Terror by killing more so-called ringleaders of the opposition only makes the problem worse. Associated with the targeted killings is a perpetual drain on our resources as the military budget remains bloated. But we hear no complaints from the war profiteers.

It is now known that the "sterile" nature of this type of killing of innocents does not prevent the problem of PTSD. Drone operators do suffer with PTSD and suicidal thoughts in spite of the fact that they are located thousands of miles from their targets. The real guilt of many is not felt immediately, and it can take years for it to end in suicide. Veterans today are killing themselves at a very high rate.

In a truly defensive war there may be a place for drone warfare, but in an offensive and aggressive war it only makes our problems that much worse.

The fact that the targeted killings are directed both by the civilian CIA and the military should raise more concerns in the Congress and among the American people than it has so far. Using drones for assassinations, including of Americans, with no due process required and with a "license to kill" granted to our presidents by the notorious NDAA legislation is a subject deserving much more attention than it has received so far. The longer this authority remains in operation and is tolerated by the American people, the more difficult it will be to eliminate it and the greater will be the threat to our liberty. Targeted killings of supposed enemies overseas, or even on US soil, is something about which we should all be concerned.

The notion that drone warfare somehow offers advantages in the current Global War on Terror is erroneous and dangerous. Drone warfare diminishes the concern for the real costs of the war and delays the realization that our deeply flawed foreign policy desperately needs to be changed.

On the radio talk shows and the T.V.
You hear one thing again and again
How the U.S.A. stands for freedom
And we come to the aid of a friend
But who are the ones that we call our friends
These governments killing their own?
Or the people who finally can't take any more
And they pick up a gun or a brick or a stone

"Lives in the Balance" Jackson Browne

15

Suicide Terrorism

Professor Robert Pape, author of the books *Dying to Win* and *Cutting the Fuse*, is the expert on suicide terrorism. His studies on the issue, described in his books, are convincing. According to Pape, it's not religious fanaticism, except for in very few cases, that prompts people to commit suicide in an effort to kill combatants and civilians alike. Rather the driving force behind such acts, according to Pape, is occupation by foreign military. This occupation motivates both secular and religious people to use the tactic of suicide terrorism in response.

Iran, a country of over 70 million people that may be considered among the most theocratic Islamic countries in the world, produces no al-Qaeda suicide terrorists. The civil war in Sri Lanka, where the Tamil Tigers sought an independent state, generated a record number of suicide terrorists. Most of the people who committed suicide attacks in that war were secular pro-communists trying to secure independence.

Whenever foreign military operations have been reduced in any country suffering from suicide terrorism, the incidence of suicide terrorism dropped or stopped completely.

Pape came to the conclusion that suicide terrorists have precise goals that are secular and political in nature and focused principally on forcing withdrawal of foreign military forces. He maintains that the suicide attacks against Americans, including the 9/11 attack, are a consequence of neither radical Islamic fundamentalism, poverty, nor lack of education.

There is no evidence to back up the neoconservatives' contention that the 9/11 attack was motivated by dislike of Americans' freedom and prosperity. This attributed motivation is a deliberate deception spread by war-promoting politicians and special interests. It will be impossible to successfully counter the terrorism threat so long as this false motivation is accepted. Efforts to prevent attacks on American citizens by increasing US invasions and occupations, and now killings with drone attacks, will actually make future attacks more likely. The more the US kills, the greater the number of people who will want to retaliate against us. Even if there is a lull in the attacks against us, be assured the aggrieved, especially those in the Middle East, have long memories.

Ronald Reagan, after 241 US military members were killed by a suicide terrorist in Lebanon in 1983, removed the remaining US troops from the area. When Israel and the United States backed off, all suicide incidents ended in Lebanon. This was one huge learning experience for Reagan who wrote in his memoirs of how irrational the people and the politics of the region were. Reagan noted that "the sending of the marines to Beirut was the source of my greatest regret and my greatest sorrow as president."

It is more difficult to deal with the dangers of suicide terrorism if the actual motivation to engage in it is denied or not understood. US government policy is not crafted to reduce the motivation for terrorist attacks. Instead, the policy generates greater motivation for such attacks. So long as this remains the case, it is certain that the Global War on Terror can't make us safer and will in time result in more attacks on us. The US government's emphasis on drone operations in place of invading and occupying certain countries will not serve to avoid the resentment that builds with US persistence in maintaining an empire at the expense of many innocent people in foreign lands.

The solution to the danger of suicide terrorism cannot be found in merely altering our intervention in foreign countries. It can only come with accepting the principles of a noninterventionist foreign policy.

Take all you overgrown infants away somewhere
And build them a home, a little place of their own
The Fletcher Memorial
Home for Incurable Tyrants and Kings
"The Fletcher Memorial Home" Pink Floyd

16

The Dictators

Without dictators there would be no war. Dictators don't all look like Hitler, Stalin, or Mao Zedong. There are many flavors and degrees of dictators. All of them are authoritarians. We have economic authoritarians, military authoritarians, and lifestyle authoritarians. They are all part of the problem because all of them support the initiation of violence and feel obligated to do us all a big favor by blessing us with mandates. Authoritarians like dependency and use government to exert their power and force their opinions on others.

Even with the advancement of society we continue to have "wars and rumors of war" as was prophesied. Yet I believe it's possible for mankind to mature and "evolve" for the better, ushering in an age when fewer wars will be fought. While we'll never rid the world of the monsters who live to rule others while suffering no remorse for the wars they instigate and rationalize, we can take action to keep the dictators from gaining great power.

The evil and needless suffering that the dictators cause never influences the warmongers to change their minds about human relations. Can one imagine a Dick Cheney, a Donald Rumsfeld, a John McCain, a Lindsey Graham, or a Joe Lieberman ever giving up his neoconservative beliefs and seeking peaceful solutions for the world's problems rather than constantly advocating war? This goes for all the dictators of the world, current and past. They know best! They are the boss! The people aren't smart enough about matters of vital importance like war, the dictators believe; the dictators will take care of us. This attitude is characteristic of economic dictators as well as dictators advancing foreign intervention. Look at what's happened to this country in the last several decades with policies of expansive foreign and economic intervention supported by Democratic and Republican politicians and all branches of government.

Dictators, big and small

Dictators come in all sizes and shape. The many varieties of dictators, both big and small, are encouraged by the dependent masses who believe the lies the dictators and their facilitators trumpet persistently. Too many people believe a "free lunch" is just around the corner. If the people don't have a strong government to protect them from domestic and foreign threats, they reason, how can they possibly be safe, secure, and well fed?

Most dictators gain support of the people by deception. Those who want to run our lives, always for "noble" reasons of course, deceive the people, and even themselves at times. The little dictators are local government officials. They start out with minor regulations of our persons and property. The worst kind of dictators is the tyrant of the Hitler, Stalin, and Mao Zedong variety. But, no matter how big or small dictators are, they all accept 100 percent the principle that granting government authority to manipulate our lives and control our property is legitimate and morally acceptable. Though it may be supposed a simple matter to contain their dictatorial urges, government power and its corruption tends to grow in spite of all efforts made to place barriers to the rise of dictators.

Most believers in limiting the government's use of aggression who seek positions of political influence yield to the temptation to use government to solve many problems of the world. Their attitude about the role of government quickly changes once they're in office.

Dictators, whether central economic planners, warmongers, or both, often see themselves as equalizers. They justify their use of force as only to help the weak, the sick, the hungry, the poor, and the unfortunate. But, most problems that political power holders argue it is their obligation to solve were created by previous government actions. This causes the bureaucratic system and profiteering special interests to metastasize. What really happens? Government grows, money rules, and the largess feeds into a culture of dependency. The three percent in need, with government benevolence, become six percent then 12 percent and grows continuously until the government goes broke and poverty engulfs the entire society as we have witnessed in Detroit. The perpetrators of the disaster scream that the only solution is more government benevolence.

Government has no moral authority to compromise the principle of nonaggression. And the people have no moral authority to use government force to give themselves benefits. Accept these two principles and the dictators lose their power. The whole welfare-warfare process is justified by the acceptance of a well-intentioned humanitarianism. But, if the people refuse to pay, the heavy hand of government threatens their life and liberty. How can that be true humanitarianism? The mandate is to be a good "humanitarian" and help other people or suffer the consequences. It is the opposite of charity. The bizarre aspect of this is that the subjects of all the dictators have generally been obedient, with many believing that there really is a "free lunch."

Though all dictators endorse the same principle of government aggression to suppress people's liberty, some dictators are harder to detect than others. A slick neocon can seem virtuous compared to a Hitler, yet still endorse invasion and the slaughter of innocent people. An economic planner might mask himself as a benevolent leader yet cause the poverty that will then be fought with even more government aggression, causing expanded poverty and loss of liberty.

Whether it's the local planning commission or the United Nations, the problem is the same. The dictators claim they will be the equalizers for all the inequities of mankind and the excesses that result from "too much" freedom. What they ignore is the fact that the interference in the free interactions of people makes inequities worse. The rich get richer and the poor get poorer as corruption explodes. Today's conditions verify this.

Equal justice is forgotten in our current judicial system. Wealth, power, and prestige protect the ruling class. The counterfeiters, the warmongers, and the thieves who steal from the treasury go free. Our prisons are filled will nonviolent drug users and disproportionately by minorities and the poor.

Today America's dictators, elected or appointed, as well as a significant part of our media, tell us war is required to keep us safe, protect our freedoms, defend the Constitution, and care for the people of the world. Military force is used against those who don't obey the US government. Economic coercion is also used for disciplining those who resist our government's commands. There are bribes for those, both foreign and domestic, who go along with our dictators' desires and thus receive economic benefits extracted from others through tax theft and currency debasement.

Challenging the dictators

Most of the people in all societies want peace and prosperity, not war and suffering. The most important thing is for the people to become knowledgeable enough to resist the propaganda that creates enough fear that the people go along with war and forced wealth redistribution.

Challenging the dictators requires the people to pursue three actions: (1) Keep the dictators out of government; (2) Limit the power of government; and (3) Refuse to pay for or fight in wars. Wars, no matter the size and scope, end when the money runs out. Wouldn't it make more sense to recognize this and deny the money before the useless wars lacking a real defensive justification begin? If these simple rules had been followed for the last 65 years as US policy, not one American soldier would have died in battle. No Korea, Vietnam, Middle East, nor Afghanistan wars for which the American soldier or the American taxpayer would die or pay. If we can't win the wars of aggression, why not just avoid them entirely? Besides, they are all morally wrong.

Dictators will always be a problem, but their potential destruction can be minimized if we keep them away from command of armies, navies, air forces, missiles, submarines, and drones. Keep the dictators out of government and their dangerous inclinations will be more easily contained.

The bedrock to support these changes is made up of education that builds confidence in a firm belief that a more peaceful world can be achieved.

How did the American people ever reach this point where they believe that US aggression in the Middle East will make us safe when it does the opposite? How did the American people ever reach the point where they believe that fighting unconstitutional wars is required to protect our freedoms and our Constitution? Why do we allow the NSA, CIA, FBI, TSA, etc. to destroy our liberty at home, as part of the Global War on Terror, with a pretext that they are preserving our liberty?

Why are the lying politicians reelected and allowed to bankrupt our country, destroy our money, and enter wars without the proper consent? Why do the American people suffer in silence and not scream "Enough is enough!"? We've had enough of the "humanitarian do-gooders" and the proponents of "American exceptionalism" who give us nothing but war, economic suffering, and less freedom. This can and must be stopped.

Propaganda by the US government and special interests that gain from foreign intervention and forced redistribution is largely to blame. Education is beginning to overcome the decades of propaganda. More education in needed.

A little truth would help. It starts with rewarding those with experience in the government who blow the whistle and inform us of what is happening. The government seeks to prosecute them as traitors, but more and more Americans and people around the world are praising these whistle-blowers as patriots. It has been said that the truth can make us free. It's about time we tried it and found out. If not totally free at least it would make us a lot better off than we are with the consequence of the lies that we've had to live with for so long.

Recognizing the truth and getting others to understand it is no easy matter. Official propaganda by the state is a powerful weapon to overcome. Striving for truth is worthwhile, and any challenge to the deception and fraud has value whether truth is totally vindicated or not.

One of the most serious crimes that an American citizen can commit is to lie to a government official under oath. But it is not considered a crime for government officials, who have sworn an oath to uphold the Constitution, to lie to the people and flaunt the Constitution. In my opinion the latter is much worse than the former.

Apathy about dictators

Dictators do not exercise military power and seek conquests only to satisfy their own egos. Many are driven in their intervention, in their eyes, to make society just and fair. Believing in their own superiority and fortified by false economic theories, dictators justify in their own minds using coercion to regulate, dictate, control, inflate, deficit finance, and do all the things that constitute central economic planning. War and welfare drive or justify all dictators—always claiming that their motivation is to keep everyone safe and well-fed. Protecting liberty is not high on the list of priorities. Yet the policies to which they resort always punish the poor and middle class and reward the privileged rich who adapt quite well to dictators of all stripes. From crony capitalism to bleeding-heart liberalism to compassionate populism to fascism to socialism to communism, the elites adapt.

It's easy to understand the twisted logic of a dictator. What is more difficult to understand is the people's apathy toward dictators and tolerance of being manipulated. The people often even allow themselves to be convinced, by those who promote a distorted view of patriotism, to support policies that are very harmful to the people's wellbeing.

Rarely are the important differences understood between the dictator and the person who accumulates wealth through providing goods or services in the market without any special benefits of government power. The former is an outrage and deserves punishment. The latter should be welcomed and encouraged. Too often criticism is equally directed toward both types of person instead of condemning only those who unfairly accumulate wealth and power by obtaining special benefits from government. Both big government conservatives and big government liberals are guilty of this abuse, with both groups reaping material benefits from the welfare-warfare state.

Throwing out the dictators

No one should be surprised by what dictators do once they gain political power. Almost always they communicate their beliefs and intentions before gaining power. Should the world have been surprised by the actions of Hitler, Mussolini, Stalin, Mao Zedong, Pol Pot, and any other authoritarians who wrote and talked about a belief system that acknowledges the use of power to control and mold the people?

What about authoritarianism in a Western democracy? Though it may be less threatening in some ways, the harm it creates can be quite extensive. Have not our presidents, whether Republican or Democrat, for the last century, even with their smooth talk and promises, let us know how they intended to use government power as they saw fit to control personal behavior and promote war?

Why should anyone be surprised that we suffer as our leaders continue to pursue illegal wars, restrict liberty, and give us an economy that continues to deteriorate as the middle class shrinks?

Generally our elected leaders are not referred to as dictators. Nevertheless, they are dictators, though of a different stripe than other dictators. In spite of the dictators' pretense of benevolence, many innocent people suffer and die as a result of US military presence around the world.

The longer the dictators are in charge, the more arrogant they become and the greater the danger the people face.

The dictators are few in number compared to the large majority of the people who fall in line and obey. What is it that makes the masses so willing to accept the dictates of their rulers?

Why does it take so long for people to resist and finally overthrow their dictators? That is the hardest part to comprehend. There are no benefits for the people in tolerating the few in numbers who are allowed to gain power and rule. The numbers tell us the few who seek this immoral power over others can be prohibited from gaining it.

As of now perceptions don't favor our side. Unfortunately the masses believe the lies, are misled, and have become apathetic to education needed for understanding the reasons for becoming noncompliant with the authoritarians who have gained control over us. For us to win, that attitude must change.

The Founders made an attempt to prevent the catastrophe we're facing. Their sincere effort to protect liberty with a republican form of government has failed. The very clear conclusion expressed in the last paragraph of the Declaration of Independence states that the "United Colonies are, and of Right ought to be Free and Independent States" that come together only in a very limited fashion. This principle of independent states was mentioned three times in the concluding paragraph, emphasizing the purpose of the Declaration of Independence and the American Revolution. Unfortunately, the Constitution weakened this important point made in the Declaration of Independence, and, over the years, constitutional constraints have not done much to protect the states as "free and independent." Further erosion occurred as a consequence of the Civil War.

And in many ways it's been downhill ever since for the protection of liberty for which the colonists fought and died. As this trend has continued, the executive branch has grown in power and scope.

Every day we hear of more abuse of our liberty by our current dictators in charge. To reverse this long trend, the people must accept a modern-day desire for overthrowing the tyranny we have come to endure. The threats and ironfisted actions of our authoritarian masters must not intimidate us. Instead, they should embolden us to peacefully resist and reject the philosophy of interventionism.

Education is crucial to providing confidence in the people that only a free society can produce peace and prosperity. Ignorance and acceptance of the false promises of the economic planners and proponents of war must be reversed. Brainwashing of our children by national and sometimes international governments must be rejected. The responsibility for educating children resides in their parents, not in the state. When the state controls what is taught and how, that's not education, that's indoctrination.

Threats and bribes by government officials for the people to fall in line must be rejected. Threats of punishment for not capitulating to the mandates are morally wrong. Bribing with benefits is immoral and also illusionary. Governments can't provide any benefit to one person without first stealing it from another through taxes, seizure, borrowing, or debasing the currency. All of these are wrong and hurt the poor while helping the ruling class. Promises are eventually not fulfilled because the governments that promise these perpetual miracles eventually plunge into bankruptcy as we have seen so often throughout history. Nations around the world, including the United States, are now facing the threat of bankruptcy.

Authoritarian systems ultimately fail as their operation

through the initiation of force destroys liberty and wealth. Freedom, in contrast, must spread through persuasion. People must understand how freedom works and why it's the system that offers the greatest chance for peace and prosperity.

Persuasion and education must be the tools for ridding ourselves of the overlords. Violence begets violence. Noncompliance and peaceful civil disobedience can work when there is an awakening of the people. Today we are seeing that awakening around the world. Placing more restraints on the dictators should be the goal we seek.

Why volunteer to fight in wars that contribute nothing for our security and undermine our Constitution? More and more Americans are beginning to realize that the government has little to do with "defending our freedoms" or stopping terrorism.

Starving the beast will one day be the ultimate weapon we use to defend ourselves.

The authoritarian system of big government in the US will end because of all of its shortcomings. The time will come when the more money they print—since they will no longer be able to borrow, the less real money they'll have.

A uniting mission for antigovernment movements

Public opinion must eventually support rejecting the false promises, destructive wars, and economic stagnation that the politicians have given us. For centuries, and even millennia, the people have endured the dictates of the few over the many. But the world is ripe for a change in the understanding of the purpose of government and for a decision on what the proper size and scope of government ought to be.

The authoritarians only believe in the rule of elites—the ones with the policing power and control over the money. The disgust with this authoritarian mindset is now being felt worldwide and especially among a generation of young people.

There was a time when all news and plans to organize against tyrants traveled at a snail's pace. Today news spreads instantaneously worldwide with the use of the internet. Plans for resisting the authoritarians will travel quickly, and the government officials will not be able to stop the spread.

The various revolts around the world in the last decade indicate the disgust the people have for the tyrants. This disgust is healthy and pervasive. Yet the alternatives offered tell us that there is need for much more education regarding what true liberty is all about and how the market can work unhampered by the special interests that control government.

Recognizing the evil of dictators is a start. Demanding change and demonstrating for it is healthy. But it's important to understand that the problem is not just evil men in government. Additionally, when power is permitted to be placed in the government's hands, many of those who go into government with the best of intentions are swayed once they are in positions of power. Even our early presidents, who qualified as being Founding Fathers, in the presidency abused the very power they fought a war to eliminate and that they prohibited in the Constitution. In the early years the transgressions were minor compared to the problems we face today. But the warning signs of what was likely to happen came early.

This need for a new enlightenment regarding peace and prosperity is suggested by the many queries I have received from around the world seeking answers. Answers can be provided by a concise, moral defense of liberty that requires rejecting the initiation of force, accepting the nonaggression principle.

In the Far East, we hear a voice of optimism from someone who has been exiled from his homeland for 56 years—the 79-year-old Dalai Lama. Though we may disagree on some economic issues, the Dalai Lama is a man of peace. He is optimistic about the future and has a strong following of young people. Quoted in a July 6, 2013 Telegraph article, the Dalai Lama says, "The present-day generation can create better conditions and build a world where everyone can live in harmony and in a spirit of coexistence..." and that "Youngsters of today have an opportunity to build a happier century." His theme is to combine education with the practice of compassion. To be compassionate, from my point of view, one must be educated in and believe in the nonaggression principle and a universal golden rule.

It may seem an overwhelming task to change the nature of government and usher in an age of peace, but ideas do have consequences. It just may be that this worldwide interest in peace supported by the younger generation is an idea whose time has come. Victor Hugo in 1852 wrote that, while an invading army can be stopped, an idea whose time has come cannot. And that was said long before the age of the internet, when ideas spread like a wildfire.

Alexander Pope says in his "Essay on Man" that, "Hope springs eternal in the human breast." This need not mean that hope is merely an illusion. Being hopeful may be a human mechanism to adjust to the difficulties we all face, but hope intertwined with reason and effort can usher in a better future for the world.

Limiting dictators will not be achieved by just naively believing we can erase their evil. We must instead construct government in such a way that no man, good or bad, is permitted to gain such ominous power over the people. And the time is ripe for a sudden explosion of interest in the principle of peace led by a galvanized generation worldwide. The nonaggression view is attractive, and knowledge of the total failure of all the variations of dictatorships should inspire people to look to liberty and to dethrone the dictators once and for all.

The masses must not be swayed by the glorification of dictatorial leaders. They also must not be fearful of their own fate if government is no longer responsible for the people's economic security and personal safety. Indeed, all governments, through the centuries, have so miserably failed at fulfilling these responsibilities. We must also reject the notion that loyal obedience to state dictatorial power is patriotic, necessary, and always good. Our revered Founders were called America's original patriots because they rebelled against an oppressive government instead of praising the king and tolerating his army's abuse of the people's liberty.

"Service" in our military to invade, occupy, and oppress countries in order to extend US Empire must not be glorified as a "heroic" and sacred effort. My five years in the Air Force during the 1960s did not qualify me as any sort of hero. My primary thoughts now about that period of time are: "Why was I so complacent, and why did I so rarely seriously question the wisdom of the Vietnam War?"

The sad part is that the military personnel who march off to war are more victims and dupes than heroes. This is especially true when a draft is in place. And remember that the threat of conscription always hangs over our heads as long as the people continue to allow wars of aggression. There still is a Selective Service System and draft registration for all 18-year-old males just in case the "cause of freedom" requires more cannon fodder to fight the wars to maintain US Empire.

Our culture that praises war and punishes truth-tellers of necessity must change if we expect to launch a new policy that will enhance the chances of achieving peace and prosperity. Our true heroes include those who have risked their lives and lost their freedoms in an effort to alert the people to our own government's misdeeds. The warmongers are fond of calling those heroes traitors. Recognizing these heroes will help open people's eyes to the injustice of the dictators' wars. Truth is something to which the warmongers cannot easily adapt. Truth becomes treasonous in an empire of lies.

The argument that our wars in the Middle East and elsewhere are fought to protect our freedoms and our Constitution is so far removed from reality that it's difficult to believe so many Americans, including military personnel, continue to accept the endless war propaganda that they are fed. Without a widespread rejection of this propaganda, the dictators win. This is why the dictators so fear the truth coming out and the official lies being exposed. As an empire builds, the move toward secret government and elimination of personal privacy progresses. And the poorer a nation gets, the more these trends develop. It ends in bankruptcy.

Allow the dictators and authoritarians to have jurisdiction over their own lives to do to themselves exactly what they pretend to do for others. If it works for them, fine. If it fails there's no harm done to the innocent. But, when the dictators are in positions of power and impose their will on others, great harm and suffering results. Prohibiting that small minority who are attracted to power over others from gaining a position of power would be a start. But, also, the understanding of the nature of government must change, and people must refuse to grant or tolerate this exercise of power that is the source of so much poverty and grief.

The increase in the size and scope of government must be reversed if we're going to keep the dictators out of power. The larger the government, the greater the dictators' power and the greater their incentive to wield the power. The American Revolution was tied to a declaration that included independence and sovereignty for each state. Unfortunately, from the beginning all we did was go in the opposite direction to the point where even the Constitution now offers essentially no restraint on the US government. World government is now replacing sovereign state finances, and monetary systems are global and controlled by the dictators. If governments are to be small, a worldwide effort must be made to recognize that smaller units of government are beneficial. The goal must be to achieve as much sovereignty for the individual as possible. A worldwide movement in this direction is needed and can only happen with an ideological revolution spurred on by a generation that sees the futility of the old way of governing. The world has for millennia accepted authoritarian government. Why cannot we now demand respect for the principles of small government and maximum liberty for the individual?

The dictators are first and foremost aggressors who take joy in acting on their belief that they have the right and obligation to tell other people what to do. The people are generally obedient, naive, and apathetic. Too many want to be taken care of and do not want to assume personal responsibility for their own well-being. For the people's desire for peace and prosperity to prevail, those who are dependent on false government promises must change their attitudes and gain confidence that self-reliance and liberty best solve our problems.

The dictators come in all stripes, and most can adapt to whichever form of authoritarianism might be in vogue. Nazis can become communists, and communists can become Nazis. Fascists of many varieties can switch to be socialists without much forethought. Controlling things is all they care about. Big government conservatives can be big government liberals. Progressive liberals can become neoconservatives. And they all can enjoy the authoritarianism of populism at times.

When it's evident that socialism is a failed philosophy, the socialist dictators find it's no problem to become crony capitalists. This particular transition has become quite popular since the Soviet system collapsed. It is doubly beneficial to those who can switch so easily. First, they keep the power and special benefits dictators always retain for themselves and, then, when the flaws of the new political system become evident, they join in condemning the "evils of the free market."

Crony capitalism and corporatism are the same and are the world's first choice today. The crony capitalist or corporatist system starts milder in practice than other forms of authoritarianism, but it always ends badly. As the wealth shrinks and the currency crisis accelerates, the infighting and international conflicts grow and frequently end in war. The greatest fear for the dictators is that the people will catch on and rebel—something starting to happen now around the world.

Some people charge that Obama is a socialist. He isn't a socialist in the precise sense of the word. He supports corporate medicine, central banking and international banking elites, the military-industrial complex, and, with great exuberance, the surveillance-industrial complex. Many Republicans who claim allegiance to the free market are similarly corporatists in the worst sense.

Some of the worst dictators justify what they do with religious rhetoric and claim they act in God's name and that God is on their side. The problem is God can't be on both sides of every war and both sides even frequently claim they believe in the same god. Not that the professed atheists are any better. They can be many times worse as authoritarians and warmongers. Some of the biggest mass killers of the 20th Century did not profess belief in God.

Invoking God to justify war or the use of force to redistribute wealth doesn't make the action right. While endorsing the initiation of aggression to achieve social, economic, and political goals may be well-intentioned, this neither makes it right nor prevents all the serious adverse consequences of such a policy from occurring.

It has always baffled me that, though major religions express belief in peace, love of one's fellow man, and a golden rule, the same religions are used to endorse war and the redistribution of wealth through violent means. These efforts gain support by building hate not love, fear not confidence, and jealousy rather than compassion. This misuse of religions must be addressed and understood. Becoming hostile to more thoughtful religious belief is hardly the answer to those who distort religion and religious beliefs for their own benefit. Enlightenment is a better option.

Only the people can reverse the dictators' assumption of power. The people will not accomplish this goal, though, by reforming the dictators of the various political parties that have been in charge for over 100 years. That won't work. The people, who far outnumber the would-be dictators, can succeed in a worldwide revolution that fully deprives the dictators of their power. But, any revolt must not lead to just changing the name of the authoritarian system or the political parties in the system. Instead, the revolt must be based on rejecting the trust in government doing the things that only the people can and should do for themselves.

This revolt will probably come in stages—in bits and pieces—and be different in the various countries of the world. For success, it is critical that the revolution's leaders must not be dependent on politicians gaining power and then pretending to solve all our problems. That's the system that has failed, especially in democracies where dictators gain their power from the voters. The dictates of the majority can define all natural rights as relative, advance ongoing wars, allow forced wealth redistribution and money depreciation, and destroy a private property free-market system. The limitation of government force is the only answer that guarantees that powerbrokers will not end up "owning" the government in order to benefit special interests.

If government is truly limited to being small and nearly irrelevant, there will be no incentive to "own" government.

For this change to occur, the following will be required:

- a philosophical rejection of government waging war without consent, running people's lives, and violating social or economic liberty;

- nullification of laws by public pressure or by state action;

- legalization of private alternatives to all government programs;

- prohibition of fraudulent money, private and government;

- peaceful civil disobedience;

- acceptance of responsibility to care for oneself and one's family instead of relying on government or private theft;

- refusal to participate in government crimes through the military and tax system with full realization of the risks of practicing civil disobedience since government will not go away quietly;

- jury nullification of bad laws, especially with regard to taxes, drugs, and overregulation of social and voluntary activities; and

- acceptance that, while sins and vices may be a negative, they aren't in themselves crimes and are not to be restricted by the state.

The determination of the people to reject government powers can make a difference. Having a policeman to break up a fight and a court to settle a dispute is best done as close to home as possible. And that should be most of the power granted to government. The concept that a government can legitimately initiate force and commit aggression against anyone or another country must be soundly rejected. Government's role should only be to minimize violence initiated by an aggressor against another person and never to be a part of the initiation of violence. The power that the dictators love to exert must be challenged if we ever want to see a world with a lot more prosperity and a lot less war.

For I marched to the battles of the German trench
In a war that was bound to end all wars
Oh I must have killed a million men
And now they want me back again
But I ain't marchin' anymore

"I Ain't Marching Anymore" Phil Ochs

17

Isolationism v. Noninterventionism

The defenders of empire are quick to mock as an "isolation-ist" anyone who suggests that we ought to keep our military at home. This term is meant to be a pejorative to discredit those individuals who believe the Founders of this country had the right opinion about our foreign policy.

It seems to be rather easy to rally public support for a ma-cho, tough guy policy in foreign affairs. Jingoism, even when it obviously leads a country to do bad things, captures the support of those who enjoy domination over other people. Pro-paganda promoting fear brings in the support of many more. The support so obtained is superficial and emotional. Once the policy of needless intervention fails and the costs are added up, support dwindles. Too much death, destruction, taxes, and inflation, along with agonizingly long drawn out wars, tends to change people's minds as they also become aware of the errors made at the beginning of the war with great hyperbole and bombast. Cries for war turn to pleas for peace.

Noninterventionism is always distorted when labeled "isolationism," prompting many who otherwise would support nonintervention to join in its condemnation. The biggest lie is that believers in noninterventionism want nothing to do with the world outside their country's borders. This is totally false. Actually, that is the opposite of what noninterventionism supports. Those making the charge are almost always great champions of protectionist trade policies and virulently antagonistic toward free-trade principles. They promote sanctions and wars that can easily be compared to old-fashioned wars of mercantilism.

In one presidential debate I was attacked with the allegation that people like me were responsible for World War II. The truth is the Treaty of Versailles and Woodrow Wilson with his interventionist foreign policy were major contributing factors to World War II. The dictators and the fascists were an outgrowth of the policies put in place after World War I.

Prior to World War II, the America First movement argued the best they could for staying out of World War II. Just as Wilson promised in 1916 to keep America out of World War I, FDR in 1940 promised not to send American boys to die in another foreign war. Those who argued against our being drawn into another war can hardly be blamed. If one won't put any blame for World War II on Wilson and FDR, try Hitler and Stalin for instigating the war with their nations' invasions of Poland in September of 1939.

Noninterventionism, instead of promoting isolationism, makes the case for friendship, trade, and travel with all countries seeking peace. It's a policy that clearly states we have no intention of invading, occupying, or bombing other countries. Nonintervention also means not interfering in other nations' internal affairs—especially to affect their elections or to support any effort to remove, by various means, their designated leaders. It is a deeply held view of noninterventionists that avoiding such actions produces an international system of respect, cultural exchanges, and trade—the opposite of isolation from world affairs.

Noninterventionism doesn't cause war. But military and political intervention, especially in an atmosphere of competing devaluations and protective tariffs, frequently does. A true noninterventionist policy at home also promotes sound monetary policy and rejects the fiat system that gives us trade wars and currency imbalances.

Interventionism's destructive power

The empire builders always present their arguments in a manner communicating moral superiority. This is demagoguery and amounts to nothing more than propaganda. One of the arguments frequently used is that a superpower has an obligation to police the world, protect the weak, and rid the world of the evildoers. An argument for the US assuming this responsibility is that it's our moral obligation to spread America's goodness, i.e., her exceptionalism. Problem is, in spite of many well-intentioned supporters of this imperialistic approach, the interventions never work out as they had hoped they would.

The real driving force behind interventionist policy is the special interests that have an agenda and will benefit from our presence in foreign lands. War profiteers and beneficiaries, whether an active war is going on or not, are numerous and varied. Interests in everything from foreign aid to protection of natural resources to foreign markets to international banking to the military-industrial complex are involved. Those who benefit are well aware of every action taken and every dollar spent in managing the empire. Many times the dollars go directly from the US Treasury to corporations benefiting from our foreign presence.

And if war breaks out, as it so often does since people of all countries resent outside intervention and looting of their resources, it's the poor and the middle class who are required to fight, die, and suffer all sorts of injuries.

In the name of intervention, the lies are spewed out about noninterventionism that is labeled falsely as "isolationism." Some promoters of war who feel morally superior when claiming they are serving humanity are instead the victims of a ruse as others reap benefits.

Once the concept of intervention is accepted, the door is open to abuse. Some argue that a little intervention here and there is realistic to help our friends and punish our enemies. Then the argument becomes about where and when to intervene and whether to go all out in intervention. Once it's agreed that we have a moral right and legal permission to meddle in the affairs of others at all, a little intervention always grows and creates danger for us.

Conservative Republicans and liberal Democrats may or may not agree on when and where to interfere, but both accept the principle of telling others what to do. Only a principled objection to getting involved at all can reverse the problems we now face with US troops in over 140 countries of the world and an apparently endless state or war.

Religious arguments are frequently used to reinforce the interventionists' desire to meddle, even if the real goal of intervention is to secure profits for privileged corporations.

Choosing a "wise" intervention in a "realistic" manner has been tried and hasn't stemmed the spreading of the US military throughout the world. It has only been used as another excuse to intervene. Just as in a war, so-called limited intervention in the internal affairs of other countries leads to "collateral" damage, unintended consequences, and blowback even if it does not provoke a military to retaliate. It never serves the interests of peace and prosperity, though some will brag about benefits that turn out to be illusionary in the long term.

Some argue that a policy of foreign intervention is necessary for powerful nations to maintain economic superiority and national security. This is not true; eventually the policy accomplishes the opposite. It grants special benefit to the profiteers and to those who understand the system. Besides, it's morally wrong for one nation to force itself into the internal affairs of another nation. It never provides greater security. Instead, the intervention creates enemies, and the resources needed to maintain an international presence end up being a major contributing factor to bankrupting a country. The Soviet system collapsed when it could no longer afford welfare at home and militarism abroad.

Moving toward a peaceful foreign policy

Many people worry about how a country, big or small, operating within the framework of a free society can defend itself from "all enemies, foreign and domestic." First and foremost, the prevailing attitude of the people must include an understanding of what true liberty is and how to defend it. Second, the desire to achieve liberty and keep it must be shared by the thought leaders and the general population. The "will of the people" must favor liberty over dependency and militarism. Third, there must be a willingness to oppose and resist the tyrants and authoritarians who know nothing yet proceed to tell others what they can or cannot do, while of course claiming the liberty suppression is for the people's own good. A true revolution won't happen if the people don't come to realize that their best interests are served in a free society. Otherwise the people will continue to accept a command society, to follow the dictates of the politicians and bureaucrats, and to support a system that always leads to the opposite of liberty—hardship and war.

We should never be tempted to intervene in a country or to become involved in a civil war, supporting the "good guys" in opposition to the so-called bad guys. Not having a right to pick and choose the good over the bad should be enough reason to stay out. Since picking the good guys is virtually impossible in the Middle East, we should never try. Even if one is convinced of which side we should prefer, we still should not deceive ourselves that the intervention will work out as hoped. A policy of nonintervention still allows citizens on their own to send money and literally go and fight if they're convinced of the merits of one side versus the other. But, the cost that comes through taxation and inflation, as well as sending off the young people to do the bidding of the special interests, should never be acceptable in a free society.

The mislabeling of noninterventionism as isolationism is a hoax perpetrated by those who want endless intervention for nefarious reasons. Those who so charge the defenders of a constitutional foreign policy advanced by the Founders are the empire builders who support a foreign policy of economic and military meddling that too often leads to war.

Free trade, free travel, and social and cultural exchanges have been systematically undermined for decades.

Our unwise policy with Iran is a perfect example of what the interventionists have given us—60 years of needless conflict and fear for no justifiable reason. This obsession with Iran is bewildering. If the people knew the truth, they would strongly favor a different way to interact with Iran.

The opportunity to move toward a policy of friendship and trade with all willing countries will soon come. Our insane budgetary policies will limit the current interventionist system. When it no longer is affordable, a more sensible approach can result. A growing number of Americans, especially in the younger generation, desire this. They now realize they will be paying for a long time for all the mistakes of the past 100 years.

Modification of intervention to satisfy both conservative and liberal interventionists should not be seen as some "reasonable compromise" worth seeking. Whether it's economic or military intervention, interference is still morally wrong, constitutionally unjustified, unaffordable, and counterproductive. Minding our own business is our responsibility. The "pragmatists," claiming to be more realistic, are obsessed with bureaucratic maneuvering. It's not wise to defend a gradual change in our occupations overseas that exist for all kinds of unjustifiable reasons. My answer to the question of when should we leave an occupation, such as in Iraq or Afghanistan, has always been: "We just marched in; we can just march out." Our various presidents, without proper authority, did the marching in; a president has the authority to give the orders for marching out.

Now that the war is through with me
I'm waking up I cannot see
That there's not much left of me
Nothing is real but pain now

"One" Metallica

18

Suicide by American Veterans

A US Department of Veterans Affairs report from 2013 states that 22 American military veterans commit suicide every day. It's tragic and sad. It also could have been avoided. No wars of aggression would mean no American troops returning from wars and committing suicide. It's no more complicated than that. Though the veteran suicides have recently received some attention, they are characteristic of all wars, even those claimed to be "a good war." Wars without end and without a real purpose add to the number of veterans who now suffer from posttraumatic stress disorder.

Protective equipment has reduced the number of battle deaths in the recent wars, but the number of traumatic brain injuries has increased. Treatment of problems caused by brain injury is difficult, and it is sometimes impossible to offer much hope of a cure.

Exposure to battlefield conditions in which you cannot

know if the next step might be your last is a major contributing factor to long-lasting stress. Soldiers are constantly vigilant as to when the next IED will explode or suicide terrorists will appear on the scene. Constant anxiety and successive tours back to the Middle East and Afghanistan are other factors contributing to the stress disorder. The number of tours and days spent in battle conditions in our recent wars exceed the average for US troops in World War I and World War II.

Operating a drone killing machine does not make someone immune from suffering from posttraumatic stress disorder. A report by Richard Engel on NBC's Today Show concerns Brandon Bryant, a former drone camera and targeting laser operator for US drone missions. Bryant was located some of the time in Nevada and New Mexico; the targets were thousands of miles away. Yet Bryant still saw the people killed and knew innocent people frequently died. Bryant was given a tally showing that the drone missions in which he was involved killed over 1,600 individuals. And not a single one threatened the security of the United States. The main goal of many considered enemy combatants, and not "collateral damage," is to rid their homeland of foreign invaders. Matthew Power's article "Confessions of a Drone Warrior" regarding Bryant for GQ in October of 2013 relates that Bryant is one of many drone operators diagnosed with PTSD.

Too bad this tragic set of circumstances never weighed on the consciences of so many American leaders in the military, politics, business, religion, and media who pumped up support for the wars and never lost any sleep over it. Many of these individuals who strongly supported the wars grew to believe their own lies. The military personnel, who succumbed and participated in the killing, are as much victims as they are the tools of aggression. The problem is that those who do the planning and are morally responsible for the war casualties often escape seeing the carnage they create. In recent decades they even isolate themselves from the true nature of war by refusing to look at, and even prohibit media coverage of, the returning caskets. They assuage their consciences by building a house for a disabled veteran, taking a ten-minute ride on a bicycle with an amputee, or heaping high praise in a State of the Union speech on a soldier injured in an unnecessary war. That is fine and generous if motivated by sympathetic individuals, but not if the motive is political. The numbers who get adequate help are miniscule compared to the hundreds of thousands seeking and not receiving relief from the suffering that is constant. For some it seems like even the best medical help possible would be of little aid. The heartbreak and pain has led to an epidemic of suicides. Many family members and friends also suffer.

"An ounce of prevention is worth a pound of cure." "First, do no harm." These admonitions, if they had been applied to our foreign entanglements, would have prevented an untold amount of suffering on both sides of these wars—including suffering of the forgotten families who are so helpless in their effort to rescue veterans from a living hell that makes death look attractive.

A sense of this tragedy is revealed in the letter written by Iraq War veteran Daniel Somers before he committed suicide. The letter was published on June 23, 2013 on the Gawker website.

After suffering for years and trying everything conceivable to erase the bad memories and cope with physical injuries, Somers took his own life. His biggest concern was what his illness was doing to his sympathetic family. His letter tried to reassure them he would be better off in death. Somers's letter is an indictment of the war, our political leaders who instigate war, and the worthless medical treatment so many veterans receive.

In his last message to his family, Somers condemned the Drug Enforcement Administration for using "a completely manufactured 'overprescribing epidemic'" to "create a culture of fear in the medical community" that prevented doctors from providing "the right medications in the right doses."

Somers wrote that he was forced to participate in war crimes and crimes against humanity. He also wrote that he was forced to participate in cover-ups. His guilt turned out to be unbearable for him after coming home.

Somers's letter screams out about the idiocy of the war: "And for what? Bush's religious lunacy? Cheney's ever grow-ing fortune and that of his corporate friends? Is this what we destroy lives for?" I see this tragedy as a consequence of what happens when good people are maneuvered into killing for no reason. Somers was a volunteer, patriotic and not psychopathic.

This is how Somers concluded his final message:

"Thus, I am left with basically nothing. Too trapped in a war to be at peace, too damaged to be at war. Aban-doned by those who would take the easy route, and a lia-bility to those who stick it out—and thus deserve better. So you see, not only am I better off dead, but the world is better without me in it.

"This is what brought me to my actual final mission. Not suicide, but a mercy killing. I know how to kill, and I know how to do it so that there is no pain whatsoever. It was quick, and I did not suffer. And above all, now I am free. I feel no more pain. I have no more nightmares or flashbacks or hallucinations. I am no longer constantly depressed or afraid or worried. I am free.

"I ask that you be happy for me for that. It is perhaps the best break I could ever hope for. Please accept this and be glad for me"

This kind of tragedy should not be a surprise to any of us. Understanding exactly what is going on and why it's causing 22 suicides per day among veterans is crucial for our future. This veterans suicide problem cannot be resolved without recognizing the foolishness, the danger, and the immorality of our foreign policy that prompts us to engage in wars that have nothing to do with ensuring national security.

Another victim, Penny Coleman, wrote in her January of 2012 article for the Justice Policy Institute website about her husband Daniel's suicide after returning home from the Vietnam War in 1969. Coleman described Daniel as "a beautiful, gentle, funny, vulnerable man" who was "a mortally wounded man" on his return from Vietnam. Little attention was given to the posttraumatic stress disorder of many returning Vietnam War troops.

Coleman observes that after the US invasion of Iraq there was an upsurge of active military member and veteran suicides and that the Army responded by establishing the Mental Health Advisory Team (MHAT). An explanation from this health advisory team was that the suicides occurred because of "insufficient or underdeveloped life coping skills." The experts wanted, Coleman writes, to blame the veterans' inability to manage their financial, legal, substance abuse, and marital problems for the suicides. This Coleman sees as an attempt to blame the families for not helping enough, and she would have no more guilt put on her for the tragedy of her husband's death.

She relates: "at his funeral, his brother gave the shortest of eulogies: 'It was the war.' Then he sat down." That's where Daniel's brother placed the blame. He didn't need the government psychologists to explain it to him or anyone else.

Veterans of wars from decades ago say the nightmares and horror never leave, even with old age. For some such torment actually becomes worse. It's too bad the troops and their families suffer while the instigators who casually and unconstitutionally take us to war based on lies are able to sleep well at night.

We pay some attention to our veterans with sincere efforts to help the amputees, the blinded, those suffering with PTSD and traumatic brain injury. But it's a feeble effort compared to the prevention that is available by using a little common sense. It is not a difficult task to change our policy and stop all the wars of aggression and thus prevent so much suffering. Just think, a sensible foreign policy could have prevented all our military deaths and injuries of the past 65 years. Not only would the human tragedy for Americans have been averted, the senseless killing of millions of our supposed enemy would not have happened. And this insane process has not made us one bit safer. The trillions of dollars saved could also have helped to prevent the financial crisis currently staring us in the face.

So often little is heard of what war does to the families of those who go off to fight and never come home or come home as a shell of a person. Whether it's a battle death or a major injury that lasts for years or ends in suicide, the mothers, fathers, sisters, brothers, wives, husbands, children, other relatives, and friends all suffer, and too often in silence and isolation with no possible help coming from the government that caused all the suffering to occur.

War is hell; there are no good wars. Aggressive wars are worse than defensive wars. Today there is no threat of any country attacking the United States. So why all the constant preparedness efforts and the spending of trillions of dollars to pursue war? Why should anyone participate in war when so many lies are told? Why the obsessive loyalty to false patriotism? And why would anyone ever bother arguing that participation by women in these unjust wars should be equal to that of men as the test for equal justice under the law? Does this mean that equal justice can only be achieved when everyone gets to be exposed to the inhumanity of wars that generate sick bodies and souls, along with a suicide epidemic? It's time that we as a country, and the entire world for that matter, reject the notion of war's inevitability.

Our current obsession with preemptive war will end when we're broke and the world will no longer take our dollars. Rebuilding will come as it has throughout history. When the opportunity presents itself, a policy that generates peace, prosperity, and liberty can supplant the policy of war, poverty, and tyranny that has exhausted the world for centuries. It's time to try something different.

Now the valley cried with anger
"Mount your horses! Draw your sword!"
And they killed the mountain-people
So they won their just reward

Now they stood beside the treasure
On the mountain dark and red
Turned the stone and looked beneath it
"Peace on Earth" was all it said

"One Tin Soldier" Coven

19

Making America Safe for Empire

Safety is now the paramount concern of our grossly bloated government. For the authoritarians, respecting liberty is not a priority. The Founders made a gallant effort to overthrow their oppressors with an inspiring revolution against the British. The Founders also sought to make liberty a cherished goal in the Constitution. Today, on the surface at least, that attempt seems to have been a total failure.

The driving force that feeds the ever-growing monster state is the goal accepted by a large number of Americans that the proper purpose of government is to make us safe and secure. Liberty is something that may generate lip service from the politicians and the people. Yet in reality it's something poorly understood and minimally cherished. This is reflected in the hugeness of government and its failure in all areas of governance to respect liberty. So far, except for the rumblings within the

"Freedom Revolution," the people are oblivious to the dangers we face. Meanwhile, the authoritarians accelerate their efforts to retain and expand their power by pandering to a compliant electorate. There are signs, however, of a broad change in this attitude on the horizon.

The path away from liberty

Early on in the United States, even in the 19th century, concern for liberty was pushed aside in favor of pursuing geographic expansion and militarism. At the same time, the people increasingly accepted government assuming the role of protector. This protection involved ensuring physical and economic security and also restricting nonviolent behavior, supposedly to protect us against ourselves.

In the 19th century the inroads occurred largely with government aiding financial and business interests related to infrastructure like railroads and canals, as well as privileged contracts. In comparison to government growth in the 20th century, this activity was minimal. But, the seeds were planted for the corporations, banking, government alliance from which we suffer today. Not only do we have the military-industrial complex, we now also have the medical, banking, surveillance, and education-industrial complexes that are violating our rights while bankrupting the US. Detroit is a warning we should not ignore.

It was the Republican progressives at the beginning of the 20th century who ushered in the explosion of support for the "safety over liberty" paradigm. Democrats then joined in to make the paradigm bipartisan. As Andrew Napolitano describes in his book *Theodore and Woodrow*, the Theodore Roosevelt to Woodrow Wilson era dramatically shifted the attitude toward safety at the expense of liberty.

Wilson revealed his true beliefs with his request for a declaration of war against Germany on April 2, 1917. This occurred in spite of the fact that he promised in his 1916 campaign for reelection that the US would stay out of the European war. Worse yet, there was absolutely no reason for America to join the war. The United States entering the war led to 116,000 Americans being killed.

Wilson, in his request for a war declaration, made his famous and false claims that our efforts would make the world "safe for democracy" and that "civilization in itself" hung in the balance. The Congress and the American people gave in and supported the effort to keep us and the world "safe." As a consequence we as a country became less free and much poorer while our government contributed to the deaths and destruction that that war produced. This war justified by deception led to a world more hostile to freedom and safer for authoritarianism.

World War I and World War II may be best understood as two parts of one war. Since these wars, "safety" has remained a greater concern than liberty for most Americans. We continue to suffer from this change in attitude. The Espionage Act of 1917, which had been largely ignored for decades, has now been revived. Today the World War I-era act is used by the Obama administration to undermine our rights of free expression and privacy.

The people placing a primary concern on safety to the neglect of liberty gives dictators an edge. This helps explain Hitler and his thugs' institutionalized killing of millions of people between 1933 in 1945. Andy Andrews deals with this ugly phenomenon in his book *How Do You Kill 11 Million People?* His simple answer to the book's title question is "Lie to them." This method was used as well by the Soviet government in killing millions of its own people.

Hitler believed that the masses were more subject to believe "a big lie than a small one." His advice was to make the lie simple and repeat it so people will come to believe it. Concocting great dangers, building fear, and creating a perceived need to be made safe by obeying the government's directives are tools for dictators.

This strategy, according to Andrews, served Hitler well. Hitler and German government officials made bold promises to segments of society, and the people believed them. It only took a small number of people to round up a large number of people. The targeted people were told that they had to be protected in a special place, and obediently they boarded trains to be carried off to their death. Six million Jews were murdered, and millions of others deemed undesirable were killed as well.

Blind trust in government was the big factor explaining why so many obeyed instead of rebelling. There was also the fact that the attitude in Germany toward guns was not that which was endorsed by the American Founders, who viewed civilian ownership of guns as necessary to stop a domestic tyranny from developing. Without this strong sentiment among the German people, Hitler readily and enthusiastically enforced the anti-gun laws already on the books—put there as a consequence of the Treaty of Versailles. The government also specifically forbade Jews from owning firearms. The system that existed in Germany at that time tragically prevented the people from protecting themselves from tyrannical government. This is a system many people vehemently want to impose in America.

Tyranny takes hold

It seems self-evident that the more authority a government has, the greater is its need to lie to the people to keep the people docile. Authoritarians who desire empire will always charge "treason" if anyone exposes the lies fed to the people—the lies designed to generate fear, obedience, and a demand for the government to protect them, even at the sacrifice of liberty. Our experience with events after 9/11 supports this thesis.

There are degrees of tyranny, from the communist and Nazi varieties to the democratically elected tyrannies that act to some degree on the same temptation to mandate how people must live and die. Politicians are tempted to rationalize their actions as needed to make the people "safe, secure, and well fed." Indeed, politicians are drawn to thinking, because they see themselves as being wiser and having access to more information than the average citizen, that they are special and have the moral responsibility to protect the people. These common temptations are powerful whether or not politicians are chosen in legitimate or rigged elections and whether or not the politicians are well-meaning or intent on wrongdoing.

Incrementalism is the technique that enables the government to usurp powers at the expense of liberty. Gradual erosion of liberty to one's own government, especially when prosperity exists, is more seductive than to an invading foreign enemy. That's why the oath to obey the Constitution includes "all enemies, foreign and domestic." Gradual change should only be tolerated when it means there is a gradual increase in liberty—a rare thing indeed. Restoring liberty usually requires a revolution.

Desiring safety and security is natural and beneficial. It's what we sacrifice in reliance on false promises to achieve these goals that is the problem. Valuing self-preservation and self-reliance is a far cry from believing the political demagogues and the misguided economists who adhere to failed and useless theories that never produce the results promised. Yet the masses succumb to promises of "fairness" and endless prosperity.

Meanwhile, the government stacks the deck to benefit the privileged few.

The desire to be safe is shared by most people. Through history, most people have sought a spiritual safety that would last for eternity. That's not what I ponder at this point. It is just important to recognize that a desire for physical safety also is natural and nearly universal.

Most people, whether they recognize it or not, accept ideas with which they are comfortable—free society is good; communism will take care of me; militarism will make me safe from my enemies. The people are rarely agitated enough for a revolution.

Americans generally see spiritual safety as being in the realm of religion and theology and political philosophy as being determined by the professors and others who dwell on esoteric ideas. There is theocracy when the theologians gain control of the state to offer salvation and eternal life through using force to impose their will and enforce their rules. Theocracy has always been abused. The Founders feared it and worked hard to prevent it. Supporters of radical Islam frequently endorse a theocratic system. Aggressive Christian Zionists also like to use the state to promote their theological beliefs, especially in foreign policy and with social gospel teachings. Zionism has played a role in our post-9/11 march toward empire, and its influence has encouraged extreme interference in the Middle East.

Much of the capitulation to those who claim a US Empire and liberty restrictions are needed to make us all safe is related to people's concern for physical and economic security. Because of this concern and a lack of historical and economic understanding, the people accept the "easy" and "necessary" solutions offered that involve expanding power over the people.

As the economy weakens and the debt explodes, the cries

are for more government spending and inflation. As the danger of attacks from those who object to our occupation of their countries rises, government offers more of the same—more bombs, more weapons, more dollars, more killing of innocent people—all of which becomes a magnificent tool for recruiting supporters in the determined efforts of al-Qaeda, the Taliban, ISIS, and others to oppose foreign intruders.

Yet none of this seems to wake up the American people since they demand more of the same policies that got us in the mess in the first place, still trusting the authoritarians who never stop promising safety and prosperity. This process, though, may be coming to an end given the rumblings I hear from a generation of young people who want some big changes made.

The 9/11 boost to US Empire

The US Empire received a big boost from the 9/11 attack. Paul O'Neill, George W. Bush's first secretary of the treasury, reported he was shocked that in the very first National Security Council meeting—ten days after Bush's January of 2001 inauguration—the discussion was about when, not if, the US should invade Iraq. We also know that the PATRIOT Act was written a long time before 9/11, when the conditions were not ripe for its passage. Nine-eleven took care of that. The bill quickly passed in the US House and Senate with minimal debate and understanding. Bush signed the bill into law on October 26, 2001, a mere 45 days after the attack. Making use of a crisis is established policy.

Wars in Afghanistan, Iraq, Yemen, and Pakistan followed 9/11 as well, and it looks like our military involvement in those countries plus Libya, Egypt, Lebanon, Syria, and Iran will continue indefinitely. My prediction is that wisdom, morality, and concern for the rule of law will not soon invade the halls of Congress or the White House. That means the expanding problems we create wherever we go with our imperialistic military, NSA, and CIA will continue. The end will come, rest assured, with a US bankruptcy and a dollar and US bond crisis.

On that fateful day September 11, 2001, 2,977 innocent individuals in America died at the hands of terrorists. A natural and justifiable instinct of all Americans was to punish those responsible. Fifteen of the 19 terrorists were Saudis. Yet Saudi Arabia was never a concern to our politicians following the attack. Afghanistan and Iraq were—big time. In looking for the motive for such a horrific act of violence, our leaders quickly explained it all: "They want to kill us because of our freedom and prosperity." That explanation was pure deception to avoid scrutiny of our foreign policy. The reasons for the attack were fully described by bin Laden. His reasons were simple and straightforward. One: foreign troops on the holy land of the Arabian Peninsula. Two: constant bombing and lethal sanctions against Iraq. Three: favoritism for Israel over the Palestinians. There is zero evidence that the attacks were motivated by hatred of Americans because of our freedom and prosperity. The terrorists simply did not like the US constantly meddling in the affairs of the entire Middle East region, defiling their holy land, and causing death and destruction for their people.

Our desire for revenge was understandable, but the failure to understand why 9/11 happened prompted 13 years and counting of misplaced anger and responses that have cost us plenty and made us less safe.

The Costs of War Project at Brown University reports that over 6,800 US troops have died in the Afghanistan and Iraq wars. In addition, the Costs of War Project says at least 6,780 US contractors, rarely counted, should be included in the American death toll. Suicides by American veterans number into the thousands and are not counted in battle-related deaths. Hundreds of thousands of Iraqi and Afghan citizens have died as well. Total dollar costs for the wars will exceed $4 trillion.

I predict it will cost even more since the total tally won't be in for decades. And it's not over yet. Even in 2013 we still had over 100,000 Department of Defense contractors in Afghanistan. And we're not about to close down the biggest embassy in the world in Baghdad. There are no plans to actually leave either country. Yet there are plenty of plans to maintain and to expand our presence worldwide as we deal with Syria, Lebanon, Iran, or wherever our US Empire chooses.

Killing hundreds of thousands of the so-called enemy makes no sense given that most of them had no involvement in 9/11. This is pure bloodlust.

Failing to understand the motives behind 9/11 has caused us to put full throttle on a foreign policy that is the real problem. Doing this cannot be a rational means of dealing with those who would do us harm. And remember in addition, the perpetrators of the wars accuse anyone who objects to the irrationality of our policies of being un-American and lacking patriotism.

What is unmentioned is the stark negative effect that all this spending has on our domestic economy. Every penny spent overseas on militarism and occupation means less spending on improving the standard of living of people here at home. Costs in lives lost and wealth destroyed without improving our national security are significant.

Even though fragile, the US Empire is still the big guy on the block and can throw its weight around. The US is still the kingpin overseas, but it takes a lot to maintain an empire, including many dollars and many lives sacrificed. Lurking in the future is the US shift to becoming the "dispensable" nation regardless of the outcries of the neocon warmongers.

Truth is treason in empire

Maintaining an empire, especially when the government pretends to respect personal liberty and the rule of law, requires deception, elimination of dissent, loss of privacy, and a fearful electorate. Slowly but surely, as the empire thrives on lies, truth becomes treasonous. We're seeing it now before our eyes. The awakening of the spirit of liberty within the people in response to the oppression guarantees a confrontation and a revolution—hopefully a favorable and nonviolent one.

Domestic changes are every bit as threatening as is the chaos that we cause around the world inciting hostility toward us. All our wars have caused a curtailment of our liberty. But, after many of the wars, the abuses were generally reduced in severity. That is not happening today. Instead, the attacks by our own government on our liberties are growing without retraction. But that should not be too surprising in a war that is "global" in nature and has no end in sight. That's what the government tells us about the Global War on Terror. And in war the people are to comply with all government demands. Sacrificing liberty for safety is expected and called "being patriotic."

One can always expect the government to exceed its authority during wars. Secrecy is paramount for the government and privacy is lost for the citizens during wars as well. Everyone is a suspect and liberty protections are ignored by the empire. The excuse is always that restricting liberty is required to make the people safe from enemies, seldom seen and identified but ever-present and demonized.

The police state

We now have well over 100,000 domestic federal law enforcement agents armed and ready to enforce the laws to "make everyone safe and secure." We also have our TSA "friends" at the airports protecting us with an army of over 50,000 bureaucrats. The Department of Homeland Security has more than 240,000 employees. The FBI has about 35,000 employees. Around 90,000 IRS employees enforce draconian tax laws that limit self-sufficiency, put people in fear, and are used as a political tool to help suppress dissenters to the empire. There are many thousands of others "making sure we're safe and secure from our foreign enemies" while our domestic enemies, including politicians, bureaucrats, and government profiteers, are ignored.

The transition from foreign enemies to domestic enemies is a natural sequence when safety is emphasized over liberty. It involves the FISA court, PATRIOT Act authority, out of control NSA surveillance, and enthusiastic presidential use of the Espionage Act of 1917 to suppress and intimidate truth-tellers and whistle-blowers. We have an FBI that participates in and encourages the process by breaking laws in its sting operations and entrapments. Plus, there are illegal seizures of property at all levels of government. Property confiscated is not turned over to general government revenue. Instead, it automatically is put in the treasury of the policing organization that did the confiscating. This process is dangerous; it systematically undermines our liberty while providing funding and perverse incentives for organizations that do the policing. This brings to mind the CIA using drug money to finance secret activities during Iran-Contra.

The nationalization and militarization of local police is a trend that one day the American people will have to rebel against. Police nationalization and militarization serve the interest of the government profiteers. In addition to Eisenhower identifying the military-industrial complex, we now have the police-industrial complex, the medical-industrial complex, the surveillance-industrial complex, and the media-industrial complex.

We also hear of internet corporations cooperating readily in mass surveillance and receiving payments for turning over information to the government. Companies that stand up to the government can find it difficult or impossible to remain in business.

Federal civilian employees, in total approximately 2.7 million people, have great authority over the people and their liberty. This, of course, was never intended by the Constitution that specified a very limited role for the federal government. Oftentimes federal employees, such as in the DEA, spend their energy contradicting or usurping the responsibilities of the individual states.

The states and local governments are also very involved in unnecessarily telling the people how to live and spend their money. Altogether there are about 22 million government busybodies meddling in the lives of Americans. This is so often done in the name of safety and economic security. For all the effort, and good intentions, the policies have given us dreadful results, including bringing cities like Detroit to their knees. The probability is that many more cities, school districts, municipalities, counties, and states will suffer the same results.

Many of these problems were set in motion years before the obsession with the Global War on Terror that drives our foreign policy and inspires the authoritarians to jump on every opportunity to justify liberty restrictions and implement the total surveillance state. Thanks to Edward Snowden and others, the great threat from the NSA surveillance is now more clearly understood. Current attacks on our liberties very greatly infringe the freedoms meant to be protected by the First and Fourth Amendments.

If a whistle-blower reveals the truth about wrongful government actions, calls arise to charge him with treason for hating America.

Allies become enemies when it becomes known that we spy on them as well, as it has now been revealed.

The state's desire to keep its surveillance programs active against American citizens goes hand in hand with its determination to limit freedom of speech and to crack down on people who appear politically incorrect.

The police state is characterized by widespread distrust, fear, and anger. Everybody becomes a suspect. Everybody is watched. Neighbors are encouraged to spy on each other and are constantly reminded to report to the authorities anything and everything that looks suspicious. "Would-be terrorists" are found, often via entrapment, to keep up the justification for the constant surveillance and liberty restrictions. National security is repeatedly invoked. It's easy to blame Iran, China, or Russia, but we never assess the wisdom of our own destructive foreign and domestic policy.

The destructive US Empire and Global War on Terror

Efforts to make America safe for empire require lying and the sacrifice of liberty. It's always done with the argument that it's the only way to keep us all safe. Denial is incorporated in the lying. No matter the evidence that shows that our presence in the Middle East with occupation, wars, drones, death, and destruction is the best recruiting tool for al-Qaeda, and now ISIS, no changes are made in policy.

Our leaders fail to recognize that al-Qaeda is a broad, loosely knit group that shares goals but is not controlled from the top down. It's not the monolith that is often presented for propaganda purposes to frighten the people.

Al-Qaeda and groups including the Taliban and ISIS gain

support because of our foolish obsession with maintaining our unwelcome military presence in Muslim countries. This encourages zealotry that includes suicide terrorism. Participants in al-Qaeda, the Taliban, and ISIS believe they are defending their homelands against invaders, thieves, and infidels who are antagonistic toward Islam. And unbelievably, in the midst of constant turmoil in the countries in which we get involved, we even make deals with opposing warring factions to the point of at times providing money and weapons for two or more sides.

It stretches credulity to try to explain away our inconsistencies in working with al-Qaeda in Egypt, Libya, and Syria while being diligently at war with the same group. Pursuing these contradictory policies makes no sense.

It's beyond just an occasional US leader being ignorant and making mistakes. The obsession with building and maintaining an empire must be the factor that makes our leaders both blind and deaf to the evils of interventionism. Certain human conditions contribute to the age-old tendency for empires to develop. Power-hungry, evil politicians are always around regardless of what they profess to believe when seeking office. Once in office, power becomes addicting and corrupting if politicians are permitted to abuse it. At the same time, limits placed on government officials' authority inevitably fail. Not conceding any legal authority to an executive branch of government may well be required to thwart empire building. The executive branch should be limited to diplomacy. Government should be denied the power to engage in corrupt, arbitrary, and destructive practices such as preemptive war and wealth redistribution.

Secrecy of government is paramount for empires and authoritarianism. The people's privacy is sacrificed as we saw from the Edward Snowden revelations of the extent to which the NSA has cast its net. Yet, if a crisis hits that requires a commission or investigation to see if the government acted illegally, government inevitably is not found at fault and a cover-up ensues. Government lying and secrecy under these conditions is considered acceptable and necessary—always to protect "national security," i.e., the state. People dare not challenge the government out of fear of being labeled un-American, unpatriotic, or even worse.

Expanding empire at the expense of liberty can work for quite a while as long as the people remain passive. Eventually, all empires end, usually due to forces from within rather than foreign invaders. Inability to finance the inefficiencies of a bloated empire requiring huge military expenditures leads to unacceptable taxation and inflation. Then the people can no longer afford the empire. The indispensable become the dispensable; the people rebel, enemies emerge from hiding, and the empire crumbles.

All we are saying is give peace a chance
All we are saying is give peace a chance

"Give Peace a Chance" Plastic Ono Band

20

Diplomacy, Not Compromise, in Foreign Policy

Gridlock in Washington always prompts cries for more compromise. Republicans and Democrats need to give in to each other to keep our government operating, and everything will be okay, the compromise champions argue. These cries are heard especially often when the nation is nearly bankrupt and there's no way compromise can generate new funds to satisfy both sides.

Compromise on priorities inevitably means more government, not less. Promoters of compromise claim they are the reasonable ones, not overly rigid and never extreme in their views. Their claim is that people who hold firm views are dangerous ideologues.

Those who condemn true believers in liberty are intense in their assertion that government intervention is absolutely required to combat an idealism that will result in chaos. It's not a contest between rigid idealism and responsible compromise. Rather, it's a contest between two deeply held concepts of government. One is based on the natural rights of the individual. The other is based on the conviction that government is required to intervene in the personal, social, and economic lives of all citizens and that government officials are superior to average citizens. The "reasonable compromisers" also believe that we as a country have an obligation to impose our will on other countries. They justify this with their belief in "American exceptionalism."

Any concession of our basic rights to the authoritarian "do-gooders" is a dangerous sacrifice to supporters of an overly-rigid utilitarianism that never compromises on the goal of statism. Just because the sacrifice of liberty comes in bits and pieces doesn't mean that defenders of liberty gain anything in caving in to the political demands for so-called compromise.

The talk of compromise between two versions of government intervention is only a matter of "my authoritarianism" versus "your authoritarianism." The real issue should be liberty versus politicians and bureaucrats telling us how to run our lives and spend our money. There's no room for a "little sacrifice" of liberty for security. Patrick Henry did not endorse "compromise" in the American Revolution and during the debate over acceptance of the US Constitution. He understood compromise's dangers. A majority vote, as pure democracy demands, for "compromise" on issues made the compromise no more palatable for the Antifederalists.

Compromising the US into empire, tyranny, and bankruptcy

Compromise between two authoritarian groups vying for power is not uncommon when a country is still producing enough wealth to be divvied up among the influential special interests that pull the strings of government. But, the interventions by the various factions that are facilitated by compromise hasten the demise of the ability to create wealth. The compromise attitude does not restrain war and welfare spending. Then the debt becomes out of control, and the give and take of "You support my projects, and I'll support yours" ends. When the country goes broke, anger replaces sharing the loot stolen from the taxpayers based on lies and demagoguery. It is then that the cooperation among thieves is no longer an option.

The big compromise that generated the mess in the first place was the sacrifice of liberty in compromise with the authoritarians who had ulterior motives. In foreign policy it's noninterventionists compromising and yielding to the interventionists. Democrats and Republicans, liberals and conservatives may argue, but they end up agreeing on many types of intervention. Foreign aid, war, sanctions, oil, and Israel are some areas of foreign affairs where politicians of most labels find much common ground for intervention. Meanwhile, the real issue of interventionism versus noninterventionism is ignored.

Not many politicians preach compromise when it comes to the First Amendment. Yet the age of compromise has allowed an attitude to develop that has seriously eroded the principle of unregulated speech. (Libel and slander are hardly examples of free speech and are considered acts that violate the rights of others.) Today's restraints on politically incorrect speech have infected our culture. The Espionage Act, the PATRIOT Act, the NSA, and the FISA court have placed a black cloud over our right to say controversial things, criticize our own government, and maintain privacy in our "persons, houses, papers, and effects." The compromisers gave an inch, and look at what's left of the Fourth Amendment—essentially nothing.

The Constitution states that only "gold and silver" are to be used as legal tender. Those who compromised over the years conceded to a monetary system of fiat as legal tender in which promoters of alternative use of gold and silver are prosecuted as "counterfeiters" and considered possible terrorists. We now also have a central bank—unauthorized by the Constitution—that is the source of much economic mischief and suffering. Nothing was gained by compromise on the money issue, and much was lost. The debate has deteriorated into two sides arguing about the pace of monetary expansion. Compromising on liberty, the money issue, or how we go to war is selling out and should never be seen as a "noble" and "reasonable" gesture.

All great religions teach, and in the United States most the people recognize, that theft is immoral and that thieves deserve punishment. The few amoral individuals with criminal inclinations see theft as acceptable with the only downside when one is caught. Stealing from our neighbors, regardless of needs, is generally seen as unacceptable behavior. Yet most people who understand that robbing one's neighbor is morally wrong accept the notion that taking from someone by force is acceptable as long as the government is doing the dirty work.

Compromising with the principle of "thou shalt not steal" creates forced wealth transfers that end up hurting the middle class while enriching Wall Street. Most supporters of such a "necessary" compromise believe it's needed to help the poor at the expense of the rich who can afford the loss. But, it doesn't work out this way. A price has to be paid for the sacrifice of principle. The net result is that the poor and middle class eventually lose out as the country becomes poorer. The wealthy special interests end up working with the powerful politicians to use the principle of welfare redistribution through legalized theft to benefit themselves. Nothing remains of the principle "thou shall not steal" in this shortsighted compromise. The result is a great loss of liberty while the benefits to the poor and middle class remain illusionary.

The allure of compromise is based on a false belief that the democratic majority should settle the disagreements. This belief limits the debate to arguing which "dictator" should direct policy and is thus used to undermine the true believer in individual liberty and personal responsibility. Instead of compromise, we should have an intellectual debate over liberty versus authoritarianism and over a limited republic versus an empire. We should have a contest between good ideas and bad.

The biggest barrier to promoting the freedom philosophy is its rejection by all the special interests that have manipulated the current system of warfare and welfare for their benefit. They ended up with the money and the power, and they will fight to keep it.

The oldest and most dangerous compromise has been between the nonaggression principle and the philosophy that justifies the use of violence by the few to run the lives of the many. Nonaggression cannot be compromised. The initiation of force by an individual or a government diminishes the liberty of another person and must be rejected outright if a peaceful and prosperous society is to be achieved. Going halfway on this principle will destroy it entirely.

This principle of nonaggression and the rejection of compromising this principle are every bit as important in foreign policy as in domestic policy. The domestic compromises fuel the passions of interventionism in all our activities overseas. The economic policies that are so destructive here at home are necessary to finance, and generate public support for, perpetual warfare. The various special interest groups that benefit financially from the war "racket" influence domestic economic policy to make empire possible. General Smedley Butler described it well in his book *War is a Racket*.

The sacrifice of liberty and noninterventionism through compromise allows a foreign policy directed by those who believe that we have an obligation to police the world, protect economic interests worldwide, and assume the role of the sole superpower that maintains by force an empire for some fictitious noble cause—like spreading America's goodness and exceptionalism.

A policy designed for peace must not allow a compromise on nonaggression in foreign affairs. No initiation of force against a foreign state, regardless of its imperfections or our perceived needs or wants, should be permitted. Neither is it morally justified. A policy of nonaggression and nonintervention means no compromise on preemptive war. It means no violence initiation in any of its forms, including drone attacks, sanctions, blockades, cruise missile launches, conventional bombings, CIA intrusions in elections and other internal affairs, or aid to factions involved in civil and regional wars. We should stop being the world's largest weapons provider if we truly seek peace through nonintervention. The war profiteers should not be allowed to direct our foreign policy.

The acceptance of compromise between a peaceful policy and a policy of aggression, resulting in moving more and more toward aggression as the standard policy, has been acceptable for too long. For the past century, needless US wars have cost Americans and people in targeted countries dearly. It's time to talk peace and reject the casual inclination of the American people to allow our politicians and the special interests to keep us involved in constant war. Sadly, it seems like only the looming bankruptcy will end the wars.

The defenders of liberty, peace, and the Constitution have made too many foreign policy concessions to those who glory in militarism and foreign intervention. One of the most harmful concessions has been ignoring the Constitution's clear directive that only Congress is permitted to declare war. I recall being told by a House Foreign Affairs Committee member in the late 1970s that I should forget about the constitutionally mandated prerequisite for war. He said that future wars would all be fought without any congressional declarations of war. So far he has been right. Wars continue to be initiated based on the desires of our presidents, and the wars never seem to end. The Bushes (senior and junior), Clinton, and Obama have argued that the president has the power to wage war at will without congressional approval. Presidents since 1973 claimed that the War Powers Resolution has not placed any restraint on their authority, as commander in chief, to use military force at their own discretion. Foreign Affairs Committee Chairman Henry Hyde told me, during the 2002 debate on whether to go to war against Iraq, that the provision in the Constitution requiring a congressional declaration of war is an "anachronism" that need not be followed. Recent presidents have strenuously argued that a "proper" authority to go to war comes from international organizations like the United Nations or NATO along with the erroneously assumed "inherent" powers of the president, as commander in chief, to wage war without congressional approval. Certainly, Truman did his best to set the standard early on in 1950 in getting his marching orders to go to war in Korea from the newly formed United Nations—an organization supposedly designed to promote peace—instead of the US Congress.

Congress's willingness to give up its prerogatives and responsibilities regarding war to the executive branch and international organizations has been instrumental in making possible the endless, and no-win, wars of the past 65 years. While none of our military operations in this period were necessary, they have together produced untold numbers of deaths, injuries, and refugees, as well as high economic costs and great loss of liberty. A no-compromise view on the war power authority found in the Constitution could have prevented much of this suffering.

Compromising on the money issue and allowing the Federal Reserve to monetize debt at will facilitated the financing of all wars since 1913. If all the costs of wars were paid through borrowing and taxation, we would not be able to afford so many wars, and thus fewer wars would be undertaken. High interest rates and taxation also would provide pressure for halting war efforts that may be undertaken. Delaying payment and placing the burden of inflation on the poor and the middle class is the option the politicians inevitably choose. Refusing to compromise on the money issue would help curtail the wars of aggression to which we have become accustomed.

Instead of recognizing the severe economic drain that war places on the economy, there are some who actually believe that war is good for the economy and that World War II ended the Fed-caused Great Depression. For over 100 years free-market economists have debunked the myth that war is an economic benefit.

International defense treaties should be avoided. Recall that the Founders condemned "entangling alliances." The modern-day alliances such as NATO and many other military defense treaties, both bilateral and multilateral, obligate the United States and future generations to provide military protection if a signee is attacked. This creates a foreign policy moral hazard; defense treaty nations will do things that they wouldn't do if they knew they would have to deal with the consequences of their actions themselves instead of being able to depend on the military might of the United States and America's young soldiers for backup. This is a guarantee that should never exist. How can one generation obligate another generation in the future to a war that has nothing to do with our national security? Yet, protection policies for our "allies" and friendly puppet dictators around the world are numerous. These policies, sometimes explicit and many times unwritten, are clearly understood. A republic designed to protect liberty at home should not enter bilateral or multilateral defense agreements. This concession to foreign interventionism gave us many of the tragedies in foreign conflict in the 20th century.

We should never be tempted to yield to policies that endorse compromise while opening the door to unintended consequences, blowback, or another senseless war.

Start minding our own business

Why not start promoting trade, friendship, diplomacy, and travel among all willing countries? We need to define national security narrowly. Current policies allow our government to do essentially anything it decides. The best summary of the needed policy changes would be to bring our troops home—we just marched in, we can just march out —and start minding our own business.

Attitudes are changing, especially among the young people. The neoconservatives are on the defensive since the people spoke out in 2013 against bombing Syria and against plans to start a war with Iran over a single nuclear bomb that doesn't even exists and that neither UN inspectors nor the CIA say Iran is on verge of producing.

Shortly after Obama had to back down on his plans to bomb Syria in 2013, Professor Matthew Pinsker strongly criticized the president in a September 11, 2013 USA Today editorial "Obama fails Lincoln lesson on Syria" for backing down and not following Lincoln's exercise of executive supremacy in war power. Pinsker's concern was not regarding tactics and management of war in the Middle East but rather regarding the president's authority—which Pinsker strongly endorses—to start a war without the people and Congress interfering.

Pinsker laments the fact that Obama, faced with war opposition from the people, sought congressional authorization for bombing Syria. Pinsker argued that Lincoln set the standard for executive superiority over the legislative branch and applauded Lincoln "providing a model for a refined separation-of-powers doctrine." Pinsker continues, "Lincoln demonstrated that war powers work best when the president, and not Congress, takes the lead." Pinsker considers this the ideal for all presidents to follow.

The fact that Obama gave in to public pressure challenges the policy of the executive war powers superiority developed over the past 154 years from the time it was defined by Lincoln. Pinsker admits that Lincoln's policy was a compromise with the Constitution. That doesn't bother Pinsker. "This doctrine was not explicit in the 1787 constitutional text, but nobody can deny that it has become our reality." And that's just fine with him!

Pinsker was obviously concerned that Obama's decision would reverse the trend since Lincoln's time toward an executive branch that could initiate war at will, despite constitutional restraints. Pinsker and the neocons appear to have since won the day with Obama starting the war on ISIS in Syria and Iraq without congressional authorization, much less a congressional declaration of war. But I remain hopeful that the American people will increasingly challenge the ease with which presidents take us to war.

Mountains of evidence show that the politicians in Washington give minimal respect for constitutional restraints. The proponents of intervention, who generate needless war and untold human suffering while remaining unyielding in their belief that executive privilege overrides the Constitution, should not be allowed to get away with condemning the noninterventionists as being extreme and unyielding obstructionists. Noninterventionists should boldly defend their principles, without compromise. Doing so provides the only real hope for achieving peace and prosperity in any country.

Now I've been crying lately
Thinking about the world as it is
Why must we go on hating?
Why can't we live in bliss?

'Cause out on the edge of darkness
There rides a peace train
Oh peace train take this country
Come take me home again

"Peace Train" Yusuf Islam

21

The Revolution's Potential

So far, over the centuries, wars have become more destructive, culminating in the bloodiest of all centuries—the 20th. It appears that war will be with us for some time to come. Yet I believe that people can change and that many wars can be avoided in the future.

This book is about the needlessness of war and whose interests are served by war. To decrease the frequency and magnitude of war, those who are conditioned to die in them or pay for them are the ones who must decide they will neither support the wars nor be victimized by them. The wars that do not serve the people's interests of peace, prosperity, and liberty—most wars—must be stopped.

Learning the truth from the whistle-blowers

The needed changes can only come about if the people

know the truth about how wars are started and who in particular benefits. Whistle-blowers are crucial for revealing the truth. Daniel Ellsberg, Chelsea Manning, and Edward Snowden did their best to reveal the truth. They also soon found out how truth is received in an empire dependent on lies. There's little chance of dramatically curtailing wars so long as whistle-blowers are punished and vilified as traitors.

Some argue that whistle-blowers are not heroes and claim that if whistle-blowers are sincere in their efforts they must face the music and welcome trials regarding their actions. This has been said of Snowden, even by President Obama. What is not said is that the lawlessness of our own government practically guarantees that a fair trial would not be possible. Manning was convicted, after months of torture and years of imprisonment, for releasing indicting information concerning the US government's participation in war crimes.

We now have a president who draws up kill lists of those individuals he believes should be assassinated—and the killings are carried out around the world by drones and other means. Snowden's life is endangered but much less so now that public opinion has swung in his favor. But that's a far cry from believing it's safe for him to return to United States or that he would have a fair trial in America. Sadly, truth comes with great cost and risk. The more authoritarian the government, the greater its hostility toward truth telling.

Whistle-blowers are crucial, but the most critical challenge that must be undertaken is changing the attitudes of millions of people about the nature of government and its relationship to the people. As long as excessive government power is permitted, we can be certain that those in government will abuse this power in promoting wars and restrictions on liberty that benefit special interests.

Changed views concerning war

In order to limit or end wars, the people have to acquire the intellectual ammunition to refute the ancient rituals that bestow on governments, which promise to be benevolent, the power to pursue war for empire and stolen wealth. It is worthwhile at times to try to influence the politicians, but the big changes can only come when the people rise up and object. They must refuse to grant ill-conceived authority to any government.

Let us hope for a transition away from war in the 21st century. It would be sad indeed if the world, and especially the American people, learns nothing from the tragic consequences of the government-directed slaughter of the 20th century.

Glorification of war, as has occurred throughout history, was commonplace in the first half of the 20th century. On entering the two world wars the people on each side, and especially in the United States, welcomed the effort to make the world "safe for democracy" and fight the "war to end all wars"—supposedly. Patriotism mixed with jingoism and prowar songs prompted cheering sendoffs. People were blinded by delusions of the victories of the youths who, in fact, were about to sacrifice life and limb in battles to come. The "big" wars ended with jubilation for the victors as the survivors return to grand parades welcoming them home—in spite of even the horrors of the end of World War II with the bombing of Hiroshima and Nagasaki.

In the second half of the bloody century the send-offs of troops to the wars in Korea, Vietnam, and the Middle East were distinctly different. There were few patriotic prowar songs, and there was much less excitement for sending the youth off to another war. War hawks still cheered for the battles that they would not have to fight, but the people's enthusiasm for more wars overseas had waned. The people started to realize that the wars the US entered into after World War II could not be justified as being defensive in nature but were instead aggressive. The wars no longer seemed to deserve the enthusiastic support that was generated by the promoters of World War I and II.

Dissent against the wars grew in America, challenging the expectation of blind obedience to anything military. Antiwar songs became popular. The troops were not welcomed home with parades.

But the war proponents tried desperately to continue the glorification of war by praising anyone who had been sent off to war or even just put on a uniform. Troops and veterans were placed on pedestals as great heroes—warriors who had saved us from some imagined modern-day Hitler.

The way we went to war also changed in the second half of the 20th century. Even a pretense of obtaining consent from the people receded.

The way the wars ended changed as well. Victory parades disappeared since the people did not understand why the wars were fought in the first place—a situation that has continued into the 21st century.

Government on the defensive

Our government is now on the defensive. The people no longer trust those in charge and the useless wars. The people are also upset about the economic hardship for the middle class and the poor, as well as the total lack of respect for liberty. This skepticism of government is healthy because the concerns the people have regarding our political system are justified. The time is ripe for ending the glory days of war and the falsehoods of economic planning that promises a prosperity that is never delivered.

There will always be individuals who give enthusiastic support for the use of force to solve all the problems of the world. The neoconservatives, though less influential today than a decade ago, will not give up on their faith in violence. Let us take advantage of this new attitude among the people and help build the momentum away from the persistent effort to control the world through war and bribery. That destructive effort has been undertaken at the expense of those who are forced to fight in and pay for the wars benefiting the privileged few.

The American intellectual contest

An intellectual contest is developing among the American people. On one side is the majority that embraces dependency and trusts government promises to take care of them. In opposition are those who seek liberty and self-reliance, while being skeptical of government's promises. Those who seek liberty are well aware of the great bonus of prosperity that comes with liberty. Though authoritarian governments always promise prosperity, they never deliver it.

It's ironic that the political leaders who shout the loudest about the material benefits they promise to deliver care the least about advancing the freedom and peace from which the people's prosperity may arise. No lasting economic benefits result from these politicians' promises. And the price paid is a sacrifice of peace, liberty, self-satisfaction, and prosperity itself.

Those who argue the case for advancing liberty and for prohibiting the state from waging war can actually bring about the peace, prosperity, and self-respect that the statists have long claimed can only be delivered via force, intimidation, taxation, war, and lies. Too often the statists come to believe their own lies and foolish economic theories. Achieving liberty results in prosperity while interventionism inevitably results in poverty and loss of liberty.

Power corrupts

The corrupting influence of power granted to political entities is a well-known phenomenon. Lord Acton in 1887 had it right: "Power tends to corrupt and absolute power corrupts absolutely." Not often quoted is the continuation in which Acton said, "Great men are always bad men." Actually Acton wasn't the first to make this point about the corruption of power. William Pitt, for whom Pittsburgh was named, in a speech before the British House of Lords in 1770, said that, "Unlimited power is apt to corrupt the minds of those who possess it." My opinion is that any and all power leads to corruption.

There's no doubt that power corrupts. It tempts even those with the best of intentions. But the idea that "great men" automatically are "bad men" needs clarifying. It's the definition of "great" that is misleading. It is widely believed in America that great presidents are war presidents. I'm inclined to believe that George W. Bush wanted to be remembered as a "great" president and that this motivated him in his effort to be a war-time president. Hopefully history will not reward him with this recognition. We should reject this notion that war-time presidents are automatically "great" when bad men fight unnecessary wars. True greatness is associated with being "good" and engaging in peaceful pursuits, which requires greater strength and leadership then abusing power to become "great" by waging war. Resisting the influence of powerful special interests and political pressures that push policies that lead to armed conflict reflects strength and wisdom. Hopefully someday we'll reject that "greatness" comes when bad men fight unnecessary wars.

The ignored lesson of history is that political power always corrupts. In earlier times power was frequently absolute, as with Roman emperors who declared themselves deities and later kings who assumed power as a "divine right." Today the "divine right" to authority and power comes by the sanctity of a majority vote. Elections, whether rigged or not, are employed to silence any questions raised about the legitimacy of political force. Though the Constitution was meant to restrain arbitrary force by our elected political leaders, it has failed in accomplishing this objective. Elections only change the process of how dictators gain their public support. Elections tend to pacify the people who have "spoken" by voting. Kings and emperors, in contrast, could always be criticized as having gained their power without the consent of the people. Elections often come down to which special interests get to rule—not whether or not any government officials should have the power in the first place.

The political process lends itself to bad men rising to the top regardless of their professed beliefs. As Friedrich Hayek declared in his book *The Road to Serfdom*, "The worst get on top." Good people, who tend to be less aggressive and more complacent, are the biggest victims of the corruption of power even though they outnumber the bad people.

It has been known for centuries that power corrupts. All efforts to restrain this ominous power have failed. Democracy has done nothing to correct the problem. Our Constitution has failed in its effort to restrain power. A new approach is needed. If getting our political leaders to use power properly doesn't work, denying power to government, based on firm principles, should be tried. Evil will surely be with us as long as the human race survives, but preventing evil men from controlling the government will at least prevent the metastasis of the harm evil people cause.

Decentralization and nullification

The nature of government authority has changed over the ages, from Egyptian pharaohs to Roman emperors to divine right of kings to the 20th century fascist and communist dictators. The present democratically elected dictators are in the process of being totally discredited. The Keynesian, corporatist, militaristic model will collapse. Government appears destined to transition toward smaller and regional governments, as the all-knowing, all-powerful federal government continues to exhaust itself.

In America, state nullification of federal intrusive powers is already in motion, and more people now understand how state laws are winning the battle against federal laws. Marijuana legalization will continue, and other state and local efforts to counter US power will follow as the bankruptcy of the national government progresses. Efforts to restore sound money are now being promoted in various state legislatures.

The chaos of bankruptcy will be met with proposals of reforms to keep the system operating in a manner that salvages centralized power over the people. Politicians will say, as we have heard them say for a long time from both sides (though from conservatives more than liberals), that we can pay for US militarism and welfare by cutting "waste, fraud, and abuse." But, the record is quite clear. That solution never worked, and won't work, for one reason: Government is wasteful, fraudulent, and abusive by its very nature. To get rid of waste, fraud, and abuse, government power has to be dealt with. Government's legitimacy has to be challenged. Its claims of success must be refuted. The people who desire peace and prosperity must accept the fact that government and the politicians never deliver peace or prosperity.

The masses always follow strong leadership. Unfortunately, in most of history those who convinced the people to follow them offered answers that can only be provided by an authoritarian government. We need leadership to advance a new paradigm for small, less authoritarian, and more voluntaristic governance in the place of large centralized government. If the vacuum that is left with the collapsing centralized government is filled with leaders advocating a decentralized approach, success is achievable. Support of the people is the key requirement. Giving up on the ancient tradition of trusting in the god-kings for protection and sustenance is the real challenge. The change can only be accomplished by intellectuals changing the attitudes of thought leaders, and ultimately an adoption of the ideas by the majority of the people. It has been the thought leaders over the centuries who promoted the government power, endless wars, and forceful wealth redistribution that the people, to their great detriment, have naively accepted.

Government force has too often been accepted as necessary to smooth out the unfairness claimed to be a natural consequence of "too much" freedom. Accepting this argument has had tragic consequences for the productivity and prosperity of the average person. The failures of these government efforts are allowed to compound year after year because of a lack of an enlightened understanding of how freedom and a market economy actually work. If that understanding becomes widely held, it will provide a welcome solution to the worldwide economic crisis. The solution will include denying governments the power that always corrupts and always fails to provide for a lasting prosperity for the masses.

Admittedly, denying to the government the authority to initiate force in foreign affairs is difficult. Pretending to keep us safe from the evildoers who supposedly constantly lurk around us and are claimed to be on the verge of killing us is a hard tradition to break. Even though it degrades respect for freedom and reduces prosperity, the prevailing attitude has been that to be safe and secure we must concede to the government ominous powers. Look at how detrimental that concession has been not only in the last couple of decades, but throughout history. The US military is the most powerful in all of history, yet Americans continue to die in a series of wars, the treasury is bare, and the US is the most hated nation in the world. Constitutional rights are shredded by the very same government that the people have relied on to make them safe and well fed. The evidence is overwhelming that centralized power, due to its corruptibility, has been a total failure.

There is another option available and necessary to choose for avoiding costly and unnecessary war.

An armed citizenry with an understanding and love of liberty can provide the ultimate security and thwart any invading force. Our overwhelming military power did not produce a victory in Korea, Vietnam, Iraq, or Afghanistan. When a people are determined to defend their homeland, regardless of the size of the threat, they are quite capable. Americans can do the same if the unlikely need arises.

Admiral Isoroku Yamamoto, commander in chief of the Japanese navy during World War II, is claimed to have said: "You cannot invade the mainland of the United States. There would be a rifle behind every blade of grass." Though it's possible that he did not actually say it, others have voiced the same opinion, and it comes very near to the truth. The fact that two great oceans give us unique protection from invasion of foreign forces also reduces our need for any significant standing army.

We could have done with a lot less of the militarism of the 20th century. We'll have a lot less militarism as the 21st century progresses because there will be no money to pay for it. For both practical and philosophical reasons, we should ready ourselves for a different foreign policy and a different approach to national security and protecting our homeland.

Even with decentralized government in all areas, from welfare to national defense, evil will still be with us and a problem to contend with. Local options, though, can be more effective and certainly less expensive in dealing with those who use violence to have their way. Devising a system that prevents the evil ones from gaining power over others is the most important course that civilization must follow to advance the cause of peace and prosperity.

If limiting government power by constitutional restraints doesn't work, and if trying to influence elections to keep evil people out of office doesn't work, what is left? Some would argue nothing. But, in reality the people can go on strike and refuse to finance or to fight in wars that have no legitimacy. For this to be fully effective the people of the entire world must refuse to sanction the wars that have no legitimacy. All governments should be challenged when the propaganda for war is initiated. Wars would still occur, but they would be minimized and more likely kept local.

The people would pit themselves against the tyrants rather than needlessly dying for the powerful elite. Continuing to naively accept and even support the wars will just kill and injure more people and reduce prosperity for the thugs' gain. The battle cry of the "universal soldier" can change. Instead of the propagandists motivating the combatants to hate a nonthreatening enemy, the people's voices can shout: "Citizens of all countries awaken! Reject government authority; neither grant it nor tolerate it." This would give the world the best chance for establishing a policy that would bring a lasting peace. The potential victims who would die and pay for a proposed war should join together, via modern communications, and reject the propaganda being spewed out by governments. They must reject the fear and hatred that the war propagandists aspire to create in order to get young people, who have no beef with each other, to sacrifice their own lives for a so-called patriotic cause that only serves special interests. Speaking truth, before a war breaks out, is far superior to depending on the historians to sort it all out, with the help of a rare whistle-blower, years after blood is spilled.

Let the authoritarian politicians do little by themselves plus deny them any funds or bodies with which to fight. Even if the people of only one country follow this path, it will be a start, and the process will spread. Massive peaceful civil disobedience against government-initiated violence cannot be stopped once this "idea whose time has come" spreads worldwide like a giant brushfire. The granting to government of the immoral monopoly on the use of force has lasted too long—essentially all of history. This authority has for too long been abused by government. It is time to end it. Our security and our prosperity will be better served by small units of government and the rules of free markets and property ownership.

In recent decades we have witnessed serious efforts around the world by people rallying in opposition to authoritarian governments. Results have been varied. One thing for certain is that authoritarians in government will resist any challenge to their authority with all their might—and they have plenty, including militaries, economic controls, and propaganda operations. The might of government will be the argument used against my emphasis on the power of ideas and nonviolent civil disobedience to challenge the powerful and wealthy elite. We can expect they will not hesitate to use whatever force they think will be effective for maintaining the status quo in which they are in charge.

We need not accept that the human race cannot progress in human relationships as it has in scientific achievements. We must refute the argument that liberty for all cannot supplant the authoritarianism of the few that has long been tolerated. Granted, success in reining in out of control government authority may seem remote if one looks at recent history. Though the American Revolution against Great Britain represents a modest victory in this effort, liberty in the United States has not continued to thrive in recent decades. Liberty can thrive again with a change in attitude regarding government and its power monopoly.

There is good evidence that the Freedom Revolution is making progress. More people around the world today realize that the conventional wisdom regarding government power needs challenging. The 20th century failure of authoritarian governments has provided substantial evidence that there's a better way. A concept of free people spontaneously caring for themselves, in contrast to a dependency on the lies of government demagogues, is ripe for implementing. All variations of authoritarianism have been fully tested, and all have been found wanting. Some changes since 1989 should energize us. They should reaffirm our conviction that ideas indeed rule the world and are far superior to the bombs and guns of the thugs who have assumed power in most governments for so long.

Soviet collapse

The Soviet communist empire initiated in 1917 and disappeared almost like magic on December 26, 1991. The collapse was accomplished with little violence compared to most major revolutions. The Soviet system lasted 74 years. It was a failed experiment from the start. It was held together by the government's armed might and wholesale murder. With the Soviet collapse, republics of the Soviet Union achieved recognition of their independence. Few people predicted this greatest of political events of the 20th century. Yet, Ludwig von Mises, the great Austrian economist, would not have been surprised if he had lived to witness it. Since even before the Bolsheviks took over, Mises predicted the inevitable failure of socialism.

The collapse of the Soviet system in 1991 was preceded by

events that revealed that Soviet communism was not working. Even the military might of the Soviet Union was not enough to stop the unraveling that occurred. Revolutionary changes, inspired by unarmed citizens in East Germany and the reluctance of the Soviets to send in their tanks led to the Berlin Wall tumbling down—live on TV. Both eastern and western Germans breached the wall on November 9, 1989, and by October 3, 1990 Germany was reunited. A few decades earlier the heavy hand of the Soviet leaders had come down hard and squelched efforts to overthrow the communist dictatorships in Hungary and Czechoslovakia.

The transition was extraordinary considering the millions killed during communist control to secure the ugly experiment inspired by Marx and Lenin. On December 25, 1991, the day before the Soviet system officially ended, Gorbachev resigned and calmly turned the launching codes to the nuclear arsenal over to Boris Yeltsin. The Soviet Union flag was lowered at the Kremlin, and the Russian flag was raised. This all occurred rather spontaneously. Few people anticipated the Soviet Empire's collapse. The collapse occurred because of an idea whose time had come. It was obvious that there was something better out there than the communism with which the people in the Soviet Union and related nations had suffered.

The people were ready, the time was right, and the system had failed. This was recognized by the people, and that recognition sent the message to the government diehards that the change that was coming could not be stopped.

Results were mixed. It was great that the world witnessed the failure of an evil and never viable system, though one defended vehemently by many intellectuals even in the West. The predominant sentiment of the people was that a new system must replace the failed ideas of communism. But, the replacement was not well thought out. The freedom philosophy was not given serious consideration.

An important message from the collapse of the Soviet Union is that people can overthrow a ruthless government even when an idea is their only weapon and success seems virtually impossible. But, as is usual for most of history, once the people rid themselves of ruthless governments, the old governments are often merely replaced by different forms of authoritarianism. Frequently many of the same people running the old system end up running the new one. The people are then pacified with some beneficial changes such as less government-inspired violence in foreign lands as well as against the people at home. Unfortunately much of the former Soviet system shifted toward a system of corporatism, welfarism, and inflationism. For a while this seemed so much better than communism, but in time this Keynesian system will also fail. And, unfortunately, if natural progression is not stopped, it will lead toward fascism.

Success for the cause of liberty requires an end to the flawed systems of government and their replacement with a free society. A new understanding of what limiting government powers really means is necessary.

China changes

Just as Soviet communism was being buried, the winds of change were blowing in China. The people were becoming restless after 40 years of communist failures. The civil war that brought communism to China started in 1927 but was not completed until 1950. World War II and runaway inflation played a role in Chiang Kai-shek's defeat, with the Republic of China being limited essentially to Taiwan and additional smaller islands.

Ruthless communist dictators, responsible for the death of millions of Chinese citizens, controlled policy for four decades.

The economic results were also devastating. By 1989 many people had had enough. They went to the streets. Demonstrations climaxed with a historic event known as the June Fourth Incident. The demonstrations against the government were much broader than what many people understand from the well-recorded violence on Tiananmen Square and in Beijing. Prior to the confrontation with government tanks, demonstrations occurred in over 400 cities. To silence the demonstrations in Beijing, martial law was declared and 300,000 troops with tanks were sent in. Within days the streets were cleared and many people were killed. The revolt was considered over. Communist dictators remained in charge. The conclusion of the uprising in China looked different than in the Soviet Union where there was a dramatic change in the political structure with republics seceding peacefully, Gorbachev resigning, the Soviet flag being replaced with the Russian flag, and control of the nuclear arsenal peacefully changing hands. Yet the results in China were every bit as historic as those achieved with the people's rejection of communism in the Soviet Union.

It is said that China is still a communist state, but I doubt that Marx, Lenin, or Stalin would agree. It's more communism in name only that exists today. China has changed. It is not a "free" nation in the true sense. It is though a much better place than it was in the 1950s when the US was at war with China on the Korean Peninsula—more of a reflection of our foreign policy mistakes than theirs.

I'd like to think the "Tank Man" had a lot to do with the positive changes since the "failed" demonstration on Tiananmen Square. On June 5, 1989, as tanks rolled through Beijing, a single man stopped a column of tanks by merely standing in front of the tanks and defying them to run over him—which they did not do. After a while he was whisked away; his fate was never determined with certainty. He may well have been quickly assassinated. His image of bravery, seen on TV around the world, was magnificently inspirational. I'm convinced he will never be forgotten. I'd like to think that he had more to do with nudging the communist leaders toward worthy reforms than all the others put together. He represented an idea that the tanks were unable to stop.

I was so impressed by the "Tank Man" photograph. I mentioned to my congressional staff its significance frequently enough that they ordered a copy of the AP photograph and had it framed for me for my birthday in 1999. It has been hanging in one of my offices ever since. My analysis is simply that we were seeing a courageous example of one man standing up against tyranny, demonstrating that even a single person can make a difference. Though the revolt was suppressed by military power, many positive changes came from it. The spirit of the "Tank Man" far outweighed the spirit of a dying and deadly authoritarian system of government. Courage by one person to confront a powerful enemy is oftentimes needed. It is something everyone should consider. The spirit of the standoff, characterized by that single man, is what challenged authoritarian communism in China.

Think of the many positive changes that have occurred with Americans' relations with the Chinese since 1989. Trade, travel, and friendship have all improved, providing a counterweight against ambitions for war with China. In 2013 Air China tested multiple weekly nonstop flights between Beijing and Houston, near my home. The test schedule was quickly successful and was upgraded to a daily nonstop flight between the two cities. The airline has nonstop flights between China and six US cities.

Revolutions can be slow and messy, but, if ideological and steadily pursued, victory can be won. Actually, with the changes that have occurred with China philosophically in recent years, we can claim the "Tank Man" won the war. Although he didn't prevent the tanks from advancing on June 5, 1989, his outstanding bravery and magnificent effort to stand up against the tanks and resist power was historic.

Arab Spring

The more recent Arab Spring revolutions are significant. They were at times spontaneous and at other times orchestrated by outsiders. This brought about mixed results in the color revolutions of the various Arab countries. Too often the revolutions were not truly philosophic and represented only power struggles and false promises among certain factions. The US involvement in the Arab Spring revolutions was of no help and made things worse. The revolts in China and the Soviet Union did not require American money or weapons. The time had come for change in China and the Soviet Union. The people's attitudes changed, and this forced governments to change.

America's Freedom Revolution

In America, unfortunately, it seems that courage and bravery is exalted in association with participation in war, while those who singly stand up to the state and to its militarism are rarely celebrated. More frequently they are stigmatized and ridiculed.

Edward Snowden, Chelsea Manning, Daniel Ellsberg, and other whistle-blowers—not the perpetrators of unjust wars and unconstitutional surveillance of the American people—are the heroes.

It is not uncommon for a counterrevolution to occur with others coopting for their own benefit the revolutionary forces. This is to be expected.

Our own Freedom Revolution—starting in 2007—was no Tiananmen Square or Berlin Wall equal, but it was and remains a significant event. Mostly spontaneously, on December 16, 2007 during the Republican presidential primary a "money bomb" event broke out on the internet to raise money for the Ron Paul presidential campaign. The date was chosen to celebrate the original Boston Tea Party of December 16, 1773. Many events were held around the country, and tens of thousands of people donated. Through the internet millions became aware of a grassroots campaign, with a lot of spontaneous coordination. The effort was truly trying to bring revolutionary changes to the government that has held down Americans' prosperity, instigated wars, and diminished personal liberty. As a fundraising event the tea party money bomb was very successful. As a political event it was as well. Many more joined in the effort to not only bring about change but also to specifically replace the failed philosophy of interventionism with one that set liberty as the goal.

The emerging "Liberty Movement" was successful enough that the momentum continued after the campaign of 2008 and influenced the 2010 election with the formation of the unofficial "Tea Party." It was helpful to the Republicans in the off-year elections with Republicans taking back control of the House of Representatives with 63 seats won from the Democrats. But something happened along the way between 2007 and November 2010. The influential Tea Party became much larger and unofficially merged into the Republican Party. The Republican Party orchestrated a "counterrevolution" to the Ron Paul presidential platform that motivated many to participate in the exciting event of December 16, 2007 and to later work to advance liberty. Part of the message was coopted and used to help individual Republican candidates who, like the party's leadership, did not support the message of liberty that stirs the hearts and minds of so many Americans. One motivation of the Republican Party was to protect the neocons' foreign policy from being challenged by the principles of non-interventionism. The message was watered down and perverted by some. But, the real Freedom Revolution's momentum for change continues with strong support among many.

Some would argue that the "Revolution" was a fly-by-night event with no lasting significance since it was supposedly absorbed into the Republican Party that was more interested in neutralizing and minimizing the message then promoting true liberty—the goal of the December 16, 2007 money bomb that celebrated the Boston Tea Party. But remember that, though the Tiananmen Square incident was a "failure," reforms continued nonetheless in China. In a true revolution, the changes will continue regardless of who claims to be the spokesman and who are the leaders. Many of the Freedom Revolution's political positions have been accepted by people who identify themselves as independents or are associated with the various "major' and "minor" political parties. It's interesting to think about some changes that America has experienced these past seven years. For example:

- The predictable financial crisis arriving and giving credibility to the Austrian school of economics and its analysis of economic policies.
- A huge and growing concern about the possibility of the total failure of Keynesian economics, with people preparing for its replacement.
- A large majority of Americans now demanding an audit of the Federal Reserve System.
- States "nullifying" federal marijuana law enforcement, a position now accepted by the majority of Americans.
- The people revolting against the senseless wars of the past decades resulting in at least the stalling of attacks on Syria

and Iran in 2013.

- Expanding acceptance of the concept of competing currencies, with the introduction of bitcoin and the Federal Reserve not objecting to it and basically accepting the principle.

- Growing respect for whistle-blowers and especially for Edward Snowden, while government snooping on the American people is being rejected.

- Developing of private technical means for individuals and businesses to thwart the US government's continuous violation of Fourth Amendment rights, including through the NSA.

- People giving up on the monolithic US government and starting to ignore it and even to obstruct it with local laws challenging intrusion into state and local affairs.

- Expanding realization that deficits do matter; the bankruptcy of Detroit is sending a powerful message.

Revolutions replacing overbearing governments are not a new phenomenon. And revolutions can bring temporary improvement by curtailing governments' abuse of their power. But, a revolution stripping government of its authority to initiate violence in all activities has not occurred. The Founders of this nation tried, but the conditions under which we must live today indicate their effort failed.

Often revolutions result in one authoritarian regime replacing another. When revolutions result in some improvements, these improvements are usually lost in time with the authoritarians quickly grabbing power and the people condoning such because of apathy or a desire to be taken care of.

The fundamental issue is that the role of government must change. The principle that allows a few leaders to engage a country in war and to arbitrarily and forcibly redistribute wealth must be challenged. For the Freedom Revolution, now several years old, to be successful, both the leaders and the people supporting the revolution must say precisely what kind of government is needed. Switching from one totalitarian system to another, regardless of the rhetoric, will not bring about the changes needed to institute a truly free society.

If the authoritarians continue to abuse power in spite of constitutional and moral limits, the only recourse left is for the people to go on strike and refuse to sanction the wars and thefts. Deny the dictators your money and your bodies. If enough people do this, the time will come when the dictators' power will dissipate. The more this is a worldwide movement the better. It may be radical, and it may have never been tried. Yet, there's no reason to believe that mankind and civilization cannot advance in our political understanding. It worked in science; there it changed the world. There's every reason to believe that a philosophy that strips government of all its arbitrary power will provide the world with its best chance for achieving peace and prosperity with AN IDEA WHOSE TIME HAS COME.

Songs excerpted in this book:

"If I Can Dream" .... Elvis Presley
"All Together Now" .... The Farm
"Christmas in the Trenches" .... John McCutcheon
"The Grave" .... Don McLean
"Turn! Turn! Turn!" .... The Byrds
"Blessed Are the Land Mines" .... Brave Saint Saturn
"Masters of War" .... Bob Dylan
"Universal Soldier" ....Buffy Sainte-Marie
"What Ever Happened to Peace on Earth?" ....Willie Nelson
"War" .... Edwin Starr
"Where Have All the Flowers Gone?" ......Peter, Paul and Mary
"Highwire" ....The Rolling Stones
"The Queen & The Soldier" ....Suzanne Vega
"Bring the Boys Home" .... Freda Payne
"Waist Deep in the Big Muddy" ....Pete Seeger
"And the Band Played Waltzing Matilda" .... The Pogues
"War Pigs" ....Black Sabbath
"Lives in the Balance" .... Jackson Browne
"The Fletcher Memorial Home" ....Pink Floyd
"I Ain't Marching Anymore"....................................Phil Ochs
"One" ....Metallica
"One Tin Soldier" ....Coven
"Give Peace a Chance" ....Plastic Ono Band
"Peace Train" .... Yusuf Islam

* Songs are listed in the order they are excerpted in this book. I include in the list the singer or band with which I associate each song.

Other songs of interest:

"*No Man's Land*" .... Eric Bogle
"*I Feel Like I'm Fixin' to Die*" .... Country Joe and The Fish
"*People Are People*" .... Depeche Mode
"*Blowin' in the Wind*" .... Bob Dylan
"*With God on Our Side*" .... Bob Dylan
"*Alice's Restaurant*" .... Arlo Guthrie
"*America First*" .... Merle Haggard
"*19*" .... Paul Hardcastle
"*Imagine*" .... John Lennon
"*Born Free*" .... Matt Monro
"*Military Man*" .... Gary Moore
"*A Little Good News*" .... Anne Murray
"*When the Tigers Broke Free*" .... Pink Floyd
"*Hero of War*" .... Rise Against
"*Bring Them Home*" .... Pete Seeger
"*Fighting for Strangers*" .... Steeleye Span

* I include in the list the singer or band with which I associate each song.

Books mentioned in this book:

How Do You Kill 11 Million People?: Why the Truth Matters More Than You Think by Andy Andrews

Churchill, Hitler, and the Unnecessary War: How Britain Lost Its Empire and the West Lost the World by Patrick J. Buchanan

War is a Racket by Smedley D. Butler

Peaceful Revolution: How We Can Create the Future Needed for Humanity's Survival by Paul K. Chappell

Recarving Rushmore: Ranking the Presidents on Peace, Prosperity, and Liberty by Ivan Eland

The Road to Serfdom by Friedrich A. Hayek

Economics in One Lesson by Henry Hazlitt

The Brothers: John Foster Dulles, Allen Dulles, and Their Secret World War by Stephen Kinzer

Machiavelli on Modern Leadership: Why Machiavelli's Iron Rules Are as Timely and Important Today as Five Centuries Ago by Michael A. Ledeen

A Higher Call: An Incredible True Story of Combat and Chivalry in the War-Torn Skies of World War II by Adam Makos, with Larry Alexander

In Retrospect: The Tragedy and Lessons of Vietnam by Robert S. McNamara, with Brian VanDeMark

Theodore and Woodrow: How Two American Presidents Destroyed Constitutional Freedom by Andrew P. Napolitano

1984 by George Orwell

Cutting the Fuse: The Explosion of Global Suicide Terrorism & How to Stop It by Robert A. Pape and James K. Feldman

Dying to Win: The Strategic Logic of Suicide Terrorism
by Robert A. Pape

The God of the Machine by Isabel Paterson

An American Life by Ronald Reagan

America's Great Depression by Murray N. Rothbard

The New Jacobinism: America as Revolutionary State
by Claes C. Ryn

Economics by Paul A. Samuelson

Silent Night: The Story of the World War I Christmas Truce
by Stanley Weintraub

Made in the USA
San Bernardino, CA
28 August 2015